INNER CHILD CARDS

Inner Child Cards

a journey into fairy tales, myth, and nature

ISHA LERNER and MARK LERNER
illustrated by Christopher Guilfoil

BEAR & COMPANY
PUBLISHING
SANTA FE, NEW MEXICO

LIBRARY OF CONGRESS CATALOGING-IN-PUBLICATION DATA
Lerner, Isha, 1954-
   Inner child cards: a journey into fairy tales, myth & nature /
by Isha Lerner & Lerner; illustrated by Christopher Guilfoil.

      p. cm.
   Adapted from the traditional Tarot cards.
   Includes bibliographical references (p.).
   ISBN 0-939680-95-5
   1. Fortune-telling by cards. 2. Fairy tales—Miscellanea.
3. Tarot. I. Lerner, Mark, 1950- II. Title.
BF1878.L485 1992
133.3'242—dc20   91-45362
                                                           CIP

Bear & Company, Inc.
Santa Fe, NM 87504-2860

Illustrations: Christopher Guilfoil
Package and interior design: Marilyn Hager
Author photos: Cliff Coles
Editing: Gail Vivino
Printed in the Unites States of America by R.R. Donnelley

15 14 13 12 11 10 9

Blessed be the children,
for they shall inherit the Earth.

To Gabrielle, Katya,
and the children of the Earth

Contents

Acknowledgments

We would like to thank Barbara Hand Clow; Barbara Doern Drew; our editor, Gail Vivino; our designer, Marilyn Hager Biethan; and all the staff at Bear & Company for believing in the magic of this project and helping us offer it to the world.

Warm and deep appreciation goes to Hannah Jacobson Nealley. Hannah is a poetic and marvelous storyteller; many pages in this book are blessed with her insight and profound love of fairy tales.

Thank you to our daughters, Gabrielle and Katya, for sharing their opinions and advice concerning the imagery in the cards.

Our heartfelt appreciation goes out to those special friends and loved ones who have been supporting us for many years: Cherie and John Godon-Bynum, Li Bette Porter, Stephen Eiring, Kaya Weinman, Tom Boerman, Nancy Vierra, Yvonne Vowels, Christeen Reeg, Steffi and Gary Escandon, Leah Tzivea Barron, and David and Gladys Lerner.

We warmly acknowledge the memory of Colleen Keating, Isha's mother, whose passing opened a profound journey into pain, love, and compassion for Isha.

A loving embrace and thank-you are offered to the inner child who guided us and opened our hearts during this endeavor. This project is testimony that pain can be transformed into a gift of love. Love is the greatest healer of all.

Finally, a special gratitude is owed to our dear friend and artist who illustrated the cards, Christopher Guilfoil—some people go further back than the human heart can fathom. Forever in friendship, we thank you.

Foreword

The universal archetypes of the tarot—the fool, the wizard, the priestess, the king—are common to all mythologies around the world. Yet, as with any genuine cultural artifact, each tarot deck is designed and interpreted to reflect the aesthetic and the bias of its respective artists and philosophers; it "works" for someone, in part, by his or her personal resonance with the art and the philosophy in it. This very marriage between art and philosophy is what sets the tarot apart from most esoteric and so-called "occult" systems. Like art and also like philosophy, a tarot system is a reflection of an epoch, an era in human history.

We are not human beings having spiritual experiences as much as we are spiritual beings having human experiences, and the tarot is a language articulating the soul's spiritual journey through the distinctly human domain. The "real" esoteric function behind the tarot is not in its use as a fortune-telling or divination implement but in its uncanny capacity for mapping out the life we are now living. In this way, the tarot is a hall of mirrors for *the times of our lives*. It reveals the formation of a human culture and the multiple phases of its own transformation and growth. Whether that is the microculture of someone designing his or her own "personal tarot" or the macroculture of the traditional Egyptian pantheon, each tarot card mirrors a series of peak moments in one's personal and collective history.

These peak experiences are crystallized in images holding great power and insight by virtue of their intimacy with specific details of our deepening humanity. The key word here is "specific": it is through the very, very specific that the universal ground of being shared by all comes to light. Attention to vivid detail is another reason why tarot works, and it does so without requiring of the user any belief in any dogma whatsoever. I remember my surprise upon hearing a professional tarot reader once tell me, "I don't believe in the tarot, but it works!" An effective oracle, which the tarot can be—reflects those processes enabling a greater belief in oneself and what we choose to stand for; a tarot challenges the knowledge of not *the* truth but *one's own* truth.

The tarot acts on the soul—those essences of a life lived within us—by the degree of its imaginative power; the more imaginative the tarot, the closer it tends to speak the soul's own psychic dialect. At a time when people run the risk of losing their imaginations (and their incumbent souls) to excessive television and mass-media advertising, we have in Mark Lerner's and Isha Lerner's *Inner Child Cards* a soulful return to the Euro-American roots of fairy tales. Before the "Age of Reason"—before Descartes, before Newton—higher learning was commonly transmitted through stories and through fairy tales. In the light of new "enlightened scientific thinking," fairy tales rapidly lost value for "serious" adults and were delegated "to the children," where they remain today. Fortunately for us more imaginative adults, *Inner Child Cards* arrives—just in time—telling stories we all can remember.

This news may not come easily to some of the more traditional tarot aficionados who have identified with the Babylonian/Sumerian/Egyptian interpretations of times past. Many will be surprised and even outraged by the audacity of *Inner Child Cards* and for good reason. First, these cards celebrate the imaginative spirit of the child. Second, they dismantle and rearrange the traditional metaphors. As general semantics theory informs us, in the realm of the psyche whosoever controls the traditional metaphor also governs the mind. Mark Lerner and Isha Lerner have accomplished nothing less than a symbolic miracle by updating an archaic mystical system to the Euro-American cultural roots that they and many more of us share today.

The most radical part about *Inner Child Cards* is how well it works, how it plucks and plays resonant chords of emotional memory and the psychic life trapped away in long-forgotten childhood stories—every picture a different story. Christopher Guilfoil's enchanting illustrations cast their own whimsical spell, as if they were painted by the faeries themselves. The stories—Little Red Cap, Aladdin and the Magic Lamp, The Fairy Godmother (Fool, Magus, High Priestess)—say it all. And finally, the authors reveal a sense of humor in the way The Devil is portrayed by none other than The Big Bad Wolf himself. This alone may be enough to begin demystifying our "demons"...

Inner Child Cards has been created by two professional astrologers with extensive backgrounds in tarot symbology. Mark Lerner and Isha Lerner have coincided the release of these cards with a monumental astrological event known to astrologers everywhere as the Uranus and Neptune conjunctions in Capricorn (1991–1995). It would take an entire book to explore the meaning of these conjunctions, but I will say that the only other time something this big happened during this century, in astrological terms, was the outright cultural revolution of the late sixties when Uranus and Pluto were conjunct in Virgo; the tremendous cultural changes seen in the world today suggest as much. These cards also come at a time, astrologically speaking, when after two thousand years humanity prepares to enter the Age of Aquarius. Every astrologer knows how every sign comes with its opposite and each astrological era with its own polarity of cosmic forces. In the Age of Aquarius, this is none other than Leo the Lion, the astrological symbol for (among other things) the archetype of the inner child.

The authors know what they are doing. In addition to exploring the traditional myths of these fairy tales, they have ventured into the future by creating a new mythos, symbolized by the portrayal of the last card in their deck. Traditionally called The World, their "Earth Child" encapsulates the entire journey of the Major Arcana in one card, bringing together the end with the beginning as a celebration of the galactic time of our true spiritual origins . . . souls struggling to be born and to embody the human condition.

The Minor Arcana has also been masterfully rearranged for optimum creativity by renaming the four traditional suits—Wands, Swords, Cups, and Pentacles—as The Magic Wands, The Swords of Truth, The Winged Hearts, and The Earth Crystals, respectively. The early "heaviness" and exaggerated sobriety of "adult wisdom" has been lifted— praise be!—to reveal the seriousness of children playing. As teachers of contemporary education now know, the spirit of play not only accelerates the learning process but teaches the value of *learning new ways to keep learning.*

The sixteen court figures of The Minor Arcana amplify the original intention of the traditional tarot by breathing new life into the educational model of apprenticeship. Through the modern story of the Wizard of Oz, the wandering soul learns to experience the "three-centered human" by having a head, a heart, and a gut. The familiar stories of The Little Prince, Pinocchio, Goldilocks, and Huck Finn articulate with compassion the formative and infantile stages of learning in each of the four domains. Three of the four archangels—Raphael, Michael, Gabrielle have been joined by the Guardian of Crystals herself, Gaia, to provide invisible protection along the naive soul's more perilous precipices. Other cards reflect possible role models and aspirations to guide the apprenticing soul on its journey, and, lest we forget, it is the soul as apprenticing human.

Since its mysterious inception centuries ago, tarot images have been depicted in tableau format as gorgeously frozen moments suspended in time. By assigning a different archetypal story to each and every image, *Inner Child Cards* makes a quantum leap from still life to three-dimensional animation as each card comes to life with its own beginning, middle, and end. This alone is worth the ticket price to the authors' multidimensional theater of the soul.

Antero Alli
Seattle, Washington
January 1992

Antero Alli is the author of Astrologik *and* Angel Tech, *and is the director of Paratheatrical Research of Seattle.*

Preface

An enchantress. Dragons and castles. A fairy princess. The wicked witch. The big bad wolf. We cannot imagine a childhood without fables or the multidimensional characters in them, characters who come to life as our heroes, heroines, nightmares, and dreams. These figures lead us to discover the treasures within our own souls.

Hidden in the story of "Sleeping Beauty" is the lesson of death and rebirth, and the miraculous transformation we encounter as we progress from childhood to adulthood. Buried beneath the theme of Grimm's "Little Red Cap" is an introduction to the stage of life called individuation. Inherent in the fable is the personal conflict we face as we encounter the duality of adventure versus duty. This lesson entails curiosity, innocence, and the ultimate crisis of facing our own shadows (or the collective shadow represented by the big bad wolf). Mother Goose is the historical harbinger of life and myth, for she symbolically laid the golden egg, the Sun, the Moon, and, in some folklore, the entire universe.

When we are young children, fantasy fills our lives. We are introduced to elves and gnomes, dwarves and warriors, angels and beasts. We learn that faith makes the soul shine, that purity is our greatest joy, and that suffering and sacrifice are the unpolished jewels of treasures yet to come. Fairy stories, told and retold, enrich the depths of our hearts from which our hopes and ideals are born. No other literary creation has such a fundamental effect on us as has the fairy tale.

It is said that folklore was traditionally passed down by

word of mouth from master to student as a way of enlightening the common folk. In a sense, then, the storyteller, parent, teacher, or anyone who tells a story becomes a mystic. The education that is brought forward in myth is a seeding that prepares a fruitful foundation toward inner strength, security, and self-realization. Experiencing a myth internally encourages the four stages of development: the physical, emotional, mental, and spiritual.

Childhood stories are a vehicle through which we discover and honor the muse. What is it to be "amused" or "enchanted"? Why do we, in fairy myth, weave our way through horrific dramas of spellbinding proportion and, in the wink of an eye, find ourselves alchemized into stones, animals, witches, or frogs? In these transforming events, we lose touch with everyday reality and, in a sense, lose our memory, so that we may be reborn. Once the spell is broken, a greater personal myth is born.

The stories of yesteryear imply solutions. They are never meant to give answers, to judge, to punish, or to dismiss the reality that, while we are mortal beings, we are not unlike the magnificent fairies, angels, and wizards encountered in childhood literature. Early imprints of rhyme, riddle, and verse become the stepping stones toward maturation and imagination.

The child's mind is full of creative pictures. These images probe the soul, unveil the power of light and dark, and unleash the impulse to understand desire, love, and conflict. From the deep perception of "storyhood" archetypes comes the awakening of subconscious forces that, in time, heal the spirit. Life's riddles and complexities are not solved in words but in foresight, clear vision, and experience. This inward knowledge renews the soul's life. We all feel more youthful and vibrant as we grow into the imaginative world. Because human beings must enter life through the gates of childhood, fairy tales will always be here. They provide a fertile meeting point for the simple, young mind and the wisdom of age.

In our culture, we have lost contact with the storytellers of old. While many children hear the tales and understand the basic messages, it is the rare child who experiences a true magical and life-enhancing change of consciousness from listening to one of these stories. The recent inner-child work that is becoming so prominent seeks to heal and unbind the wounded child within, guiding individuals back to a childlike state. From this place, whether joyful or sorrowful, a new acceptance of life and initiation are inevitable. As individuals journey into their wounded past, they ultimately find their way into the light. What is most inspiring about this is the realization that internal healing also touches the collective wound of humanity. Through our individual work, we guide the masses forward, not through words, but through actual cellular momentum—the quantum leap into universal service.

It is our greatest hope that *Inner Child Cards* can aid our planet during a time of global metamorphosis. These cards usher in the language of picture consciousness, and from this well of nourishment a long-lost inner voice may be heard again. We can all learn from the story of the countryman who was given a sandalwood forest by the king and burned it down to sell coal. We often cannot see the treasures that lie before us. Caught up in a desperate pursuit of survival, we sometimes destroy or ignore our most precious gifts. Each one of us is as rich and divine as the cosmic Creator who guides us. *Inner Child Cards* is a tribute to our radiant selves, the starchildren who live within our hearts and speak the language of love.

As authors, we know language to be an integral aspect of our future. Regardless of its mode—drawn, written, sung, danced, or painted—language, which is our ability to communicate, is divine. In writing this book, we committed ourselves to producing the finest work we could. In our soul searching, we came upon the "gender issue" inherent in fairy tales; this is an important issue to all who use fables as teachings for their children or themselves. As you work with and experience *Inner Child Cards*, you will encounter various characters and figures that may appear to be unjust representations of women and men. Please remember that in order to receive the purist teachings of the fairy tales, we cannot take the male and female images literally: they are soul aspects of our subconscious development. This does not undermine the importance of strong, heroic images of women and girls, or loving, receptive images of men and boys as a means of developmental guidance toward self-confidence and a healthy ego.[1]

To say this project has been inspiring for us would be an understatement. It has been an ongoing manifestation since our initial meeting at the Findhorn Foundation in Forres, Scotland, in 1977. It was there that we began working together with the archetypes of the tarot. As many of you know, the Findhorn Community began in 1962 with the arrival of Peter and Eileen Caddy and their companion Dorothy Maclean. Over the years, amazing stories surfaced about Findhorn concerning magical gardens and the ritualistic "attunement" to spirits, devas, fairies, and other "invisible beings" who are a vital part of the world of nature. By the time of our arrival, the community was a thriving center of several hundred people working with personal transformation, education, and planetary service.

Our experience at Findhorn was the source and playground from which *Inner Child Cards* emerged. On New Year's Eve of 1978, near the stroke of midnight, we created a thirteen-card layout in a circle, with the thirteenth card at the center. As we turned over this card together, The Fool (the 0 card of the Major Trumps) appeared. Spiritually and symbolically, our odyssey had begun. Within a few short months, we married and began touring the United States, offering group workshops on Findhorn, astrology, and the tarot. At the same time, in the womb of all of this excitement and travel, our daughter-to-be, Gabrielle, was gestating. Although we planned on leaving Findhorn in order to settle on the West Coast of the United States, our "inner teachers" created a circular pilgrimage for both of us, leading us back to Findhorn, where Gabrielle was born in the summer of 1979. Without our conscious awareness and in a truly inspiring way, we lived out the New Year's reading itself, both of us joining together as The Fool traveling on the path of spiritual evolution.

When we envisioned Little Red Cap as The Fool in *Inner Child Cards*, we intuitively saw Gabrielle as the child traveling on the road of life. It is only now that we realize how poignant and significant that choice and synchronicity have been. Gabrielle turned thirteen the year *Inner Child Cards* was published, which occurred thirteen years following our initiation into the tarot together. These years parallel the number of cards in our first reading. We share this with you because it is an example of how a tarot reading can literally become a life experience if we are courageous enough to live out its story.

It seems lifetimes ago that we left Findhorn. We have encountered many twists and turns on the path—some painful, some joyous, all offering us opportunities for healing and growth. Today, no longer married, we are still linked by the golden thread of our children, Gabrielle and Katya, our work, and our vision to carry this project to completion. In the truest sense, we are soul friends forever.

On the deepest level, our children have been the inspiration behind the creation of this deck. Early in their lives, they began playing with our tarot packs. They loved the vivid images and would often ask for a story about their selected card. They were always drawn to the most inspired and beautiful cards. However, we wished our children could use a tarot deck that had less adult sophistication and more heart-centered pictures.

One summer morning in 1988, at the time of the full moon, we had a wonderful vision of fairy tales and the tarot coming together to form a deck of cards for children and the young at heart. As we explored the idea, we found the mystical force of the tarot to be a graceful companion to the mystery teachings of fairy tales and myth. Many revelations that day showered down on us like brilliant falling stars. We were impregnated by a vision and wisdom beyond ourselves.

Now a dream has come true for us. We are honored to have Bear & Company publish these cards. Together, we set free the ideas and inspirations that have been gestating for several years. This deck is like a butterfly, liberated from the cocoon, open to the light, and dancing with the fire. We hope that it finds its way into your heart.

Inner Child
Cards

I

The
Oracle

How to Use This Deck

Almost six centuries have passed since the earliest, authentic tarot cards appeared in France in 1392. Since that time, hundreds of decks have been created—from many cultures and in all corners of the world. *Inner Child Cards* is an evolutionary expression of the wisdom and magic of the tarot. To help you better understand the creation of this new deck and its purpose in your life, a brief look at the recent history of tarot cards follows.

Many authors have discussed and speculated about the origins of the tarot. Some have suggested that the twenty-two Major Trumps were giant pictures in a secret passageway linking the Great Pyramid and the Sphinx of Egypt, and that neophytes, for initiation, would walk through this gallery, inspired by the images, symbols, and spiritual presences etched into the paintings. Other writers have hinted that the tarot originated in Fez, Morocco, or some other fabled old-world city where priests and priestesses gathered to bring together the Ageless Wisdom in the form of a book of pictures or cards. While these accounts and others are fascinating, they simply remind us that the beginnings of tarot are steeped in mystery. What we do know is that tarot decks surfaced in Europe at the time of the Renaissance.

The name *tarot* comes from the French, in which the final *t* of a word is not pronounced. However, the name *tarocchi* was used in Italy. Apparently, the cards degenerated into a system of gambling and gaming. This brings up another historical fact about tarot cards: there is a clear link between the tarot and modern playing cards. The tarot has twenty-two Major Trumps and fifty-six Minor cards. The twenty-two Major cards are numbered from I to XXI, but there is a card always known as The Fool, which is designated as 0. The fifty-six Minor cards are composed of four suits in which each suit contains ten numbered cards and four court figures. There are fifty-two cards in modern playing-card decks, but most card companies include a Joker. This Joker is The Fool of the old tarot. In addition, modern playing cards have only three court figures (King, Queen, and Jack), whereas the tarot has four (traditionally called the King, Queen, Knight, and Page).[2]

It is clear from even a quick glance through the Major Arcana of twenty-two images that something profound is at work in them. Basically, there are three levels at which the complete tarot deck of seventy-eight cards can function. At the highest level, the tarot is a system to explore and understand the hidden laws and principles of the Ageless Wisdom. It is also a mathematical and scientific device to penetrate into the secrets of life beyond the three-dimensional world. At the second level, the tarot and its various symbols, images, and archetypes reflect the unique path of destiny and service that each human soul travels in a lifetime. At the third level, the tarot is an oracle or divination technique that allows a person to ask important questions and receive illuminating answers. In this way, the tarot can also function as a tool to look into the past, clarify present issues, and open the door into the future.

In the last few decades, we have witnessed a profusion

of oracular decks appearing in New Age bookstores. Inventive creators have begun moving beyond the tarot, designing decks based on animals, trees, runes, Aztec life, angels, and the like. *Inner Child Cards* utilizes the seventy-eightfold system of the tarot, but, in bringing through the magic of fairy tales and the invisible worlds of nature, this deck represents a major reinterpretation of the tarot and a rekindling of the heart-wisdom concealed within its labyrinthine pathways.

While the twenty-two cards of the Major Arcana have always signified the spiritual path of destiny for each human soul, many decks—particularly the Waite-Ryder and Crowley ones emphasizing alchemical designs—have included various esoteric symbols and images that have been hard to decipher. Part of the intention behind this was to keep the Major Arcana out of the hands of people who would misuse the cards. However, in designing *Inner Child Cards*, we wanted to reveal the beauty, wisdom, joy, and innocence embedded in the twenty-two Major Trumps. We were striving to create a deck that parents, teachers, and families could utilize without getting lost in a myriad of arcane meanings that are difficult to fathom. We also became aware that certain fairy tales appeared to symbolize key cards in the Major Trumps and that these fairy tales "told the story of the cards." For instance, the story of "Sleeping Beauty" and the Death card are parallel in meaning if you understand the deeper messages of personal metamorphosis at the core of the fairy tale and the thirteenth Trump. "Cinderella" aligns beautifully with The Moon card, traditionally affiliated with the sign of Pisces and the vivid power of dreams and visions. And so on with many fairy tales that correlate with their respective cards: "Snow White" with The Hermit (Virgo), "Beauty and the Beast" with Strength (Leo), "Rapunzel" with The Tower (Mars), and "Hansel and Gretel" with The Lovers (Gemini).

In essence, the fairy tales of the Western world, when placed into the right sequence, appear to be vivid expressions of the hidden archetypes of the collective unconscious, archetypes made visible and manifest as a spiritual path through the Major Arcana of the tarot. If we accept the idea that each of the twenty-two Major Trumps is spiritual being or life on a higher plane of existence, then the fairy tales and their major characters are living exemplars of those Trumps functioning in the world of imagination, dreams, and childhood fantasies. In an interesting way, children are being taught about the magic of the tarot and the twenty-two-fold path of destiny through fairy tales. They have been given a "key" to the treasure chest of the hidden meaning in fairy tales and ancient folklore. *Inner Child Cards* has ordered the fairy tales into a magical sequence on the royal road of the tarot.

We have redesigned the twenty-two Major Trumps into a spiritual pathway based on our exploration of the wonder and mystery of the Divine Child who lives within each of us. The four suits of the Minor Arcana have also been completely reshaped and reimagined. The suits have been transformed into Magic Wands (fairies), Winged Hearts (mermaids), Swords (children on adventures), and Crystals (gnomes). Many tarot creators have simply numbered the Minor cards from 1 to 10, placing so many pentacles, cups, wands, or swords on a card. In our deck, every card tells a story that opens the heart and mind to new revelations of the divine journey. We have also reformulated the sixteen court cards that are a part of the Minor Arcana.

Joseph Campbell and other writers have pointed out that each new tarot deck's four suits and court figures reflect the culture and class distinctions that exist when the deck is created. In writing about the tarot decks of the Middle Ages, Campbell suggested that the swords signified the nobility, knights, and soldiers; the cups referred to the church and religious figures; the wands were connected with the peasants who worked the land; and the pentacles or coins were connected with the new emerging class of merchants and traders. In addition, the court images of King, Queen, Knight, and Page were mirror reflections of the European cultures of that epoch of history.

As we were creating *Inner Child Cards*, it was obvious that the suits and the court would need to be refashioned to parallel the changing world of the 1990s and the dawning of the Aquarian Age. With our background at Findhorn and our focus on the child theme, it quickly became apparent how we would redesign the four suits. This new design changed something very important within the tarot. In *Inner Child Cards*, there is a spiritual energy and presence within the Minor cards. This is in keeping with the reality that so-called ordinary mundane life is now much richer on a cosmic, divine level. In a way, the magic and mystery of the twenty-two Major Trumps have now descended or impregnated the realm of the fifty-six Minor cards. This deck reveals that occurrence. You will see that we have renamed the Page, Knight, Queen, and King as the Child, Seeker, Guide, and Guardian. These latter words are names, qualities, and images that reflect our present lives as individuals searching for wisdom beyond the rigid, entrenched dimensions of life in the courts of Europe several hundred years ago.

As more and more people attempt to heal the "wounded child within," *Inner Child Cards* will offer a profound gateway into the lost innocence of childhood and into the joy, purity, and wonder of childlike consciousness. In this regard, it is interesting to note that a new planet—now considered a planetoid or comet—was discovered on November 1, 1977. It was quickly named Chiron, after the Greek centaur, a magical being who has become known to modern astrologers and researchers as the "wounded healer." Barbara Hand Clow has written extensively on the meaning of Chiron (*Chiron: Rainbow Bridge Between the Inner and Outer Planets*). Our experience reveals that the placement of Chiron at birth has a deep connection with the need to heal the wounded child before we can feel whole as adults. Notice the *chi* similarity in the words *child* and *Chiron*, and the link to *chi* as the word for energy flow in China.

One of the most extraordinary ways to work with a new tarot deck is to buy it at a significant moment in time. This may mean purchasing a deck on the one day of the year when the Sun (spiritual illumination) crosses over the natal placement of your Chiron (healing, Ageless Wisdom teachings), Uranus (intuition, revolution, enlightenment), Neptune (imagination, psychic sensitivity, mysticism), or Pluto (depth psychology, transformation, death/rebirth). A deck is "born" to you when it is purchased or received as a gift. Like a person, a deck will have an astrological chart and special qualities and attributes. If you obtain a deck when the Sun crosses one of the planets mentioned above, its cards will be impregnated by your own divine healing powers. (Contact a reputable astrologer to find out the dates each year when the Sun crosses these planets in your natal chart. The dates will be repeated, within one day of exactitude, for the rest of your life.)

In keeping with the three levels at which the tarot can function, it is important to realize that you can simply study and experience the cards individually, allowing each tale and story to speak to you in your heart and soul. In this way, you can also relate the world of the twenty-two Major cards to that of the fifty-six Minor cards and see that The Fool (Little Red Cap) is the bridge between these worlds. You can also lay out all the Major cards in order and see the progression of unfoldment that they represent on the spiritual path of the Divine Child. It is highly recommended that you read through the descriptions for all seventy-eight cards carefully and slowly. By doing so, you will store the ideas and images in your subconscious, a crucial step before using *Inner Child Cards* as an oracle or system of divination.

It is interesting to note the definitions for *oracle* and *divination* before proceeding. The *Random House Dictionary of the English Language* defines *oracle* in the following manner: "1. a divine utterance made by a god through a priest or priestess in response to an inquiry." Under *divination* is this reference: "1. the attempt to foretell future events or discover hidden knowledge by occult or supernatural means. 2. augury; prophecy." In another chapter, we will explore several different layout patterns, but it is important to develop the right state of consciousness when utilizing the cards in a divinatory manner.

We feel that there is no one right way to prepare yourself for a divinatory reading or session. The important point is to relax your breathing, sit comfortably, and open your heart and mind to your innermost reservoir of peace and joy. Some of you may wish to light a candle and/or burn incense. In the quiet citadels of your mind and heart, be receptive to the nurturing voices of your higher teachers and guides. It may be important to create a special place in your home where readings are done. Perhaps an altar can be set up with key objects—stones, gems, feathers, photographs, special mementos. Create a process and a ritual that feels right to you.

Here is another key point about using *Inner Child Cards* for divination purposes: you can read your own cards, read cards for a friend, family member, or client, or have someone else read the cards for you. Some traditional authorities have warned against doing a reading for yourself, however, it is fine to do this as long as you accent objectivity and maintain a reverent mental and spiritual attitude. If you have a key question that needs to be answered, write it down and keep it in front of you. You may also want to take notes as you turn up the cards or even make a cassette tape of your session. Allow your mind to "free associate" as cards appear. If an elderly male figure in a card looks like your grandfather, don't doubt that connection. Perhaps your kindhearted and sensitive grandfather is an important image and inner archetype for you that you need to understand right now. If a little girl or boy reminds you of a daughter, son, or yourself as a child, follow that intuitive flash. It may mean something that will eventually unlock an underworld treasure.

Most of all, feel free to create an entire story from your reading. You can weave all the cards together into a plot, a novel, or an adventure. You can find the answers to the most challenging questions as long as you believe in yourself and your spiritual life destiny. Also, realize that the more you work and play with *Inner Child Cards*, the more powerful your intuition will become. If you are not focusing on a single area of your life, the reading will touch upon many facets of your current experience. Remember to see the deck as a friend, and then your reading will be an imaginative and psychic mirroring of your inner self and changing reality.

How you store the cards is also important. We support the idea of protecting your deck by wrapping it inside a silk scarf or placing it inside an embroidered silk bag. You may also enjoy placing the deck within a beautiful carved box that carries special memories for you.

Using the Deck with Children

When you are using these cards with children, we recommend simplicity and encourage you to be creative and imaginative. Our goal in designing this deck has been to awaken the innocence and wonder of a child's heart. There are many ways that you can "play" with these cards. Here are a few ideas and suggestions about how to bring these seventy-eight stories to life for young people.

Children are tactile and physical. They love to examine and touch the world around them. The cards provide a powerful vehicle for them to explore their fertile imaginations. The simple act of shuffling and holding the cards can invoke their curiosity and fascination. As you introduce the deck to children, be sure to describe the cards' special and precious qualities as pictorial friends, teachers, and guides. This will enhance the children's feeling of respect as they learn to play with and attune to the colorful and fanciful visions that are offered throughout the deck.

These cards can be used as a quiet and meditative tool or as a medium to invoke fun and activity. We hope they will encourage storytelling and visualization. In a era of high-tech television and video, the children of Western culture have had their dreams and visions handed to them on a "silver screen." Their urge to produce magic and participate in creative play has been replaced by passivity. For many children, the inventive process of imagination has become a mere spectator sport. We hope to reintroduce the concept that each one of us carries the divine fire of creative passion within us. It is in the act of expressing our dreams that we fulfill the potential of our personal art.

There are many ways to introduce the cards to a child. You can fan the twenty-two Major Arcana cards out in an arc and have the child choose one. The chosen card then becomes the story that you share together. You can lay out all seventy-eight cards and have the child choose from the entire deck. Any image that appears can be the idea for a story or play. Encourage children to invent and discover their own meanings behind each card. At first they may resist. This is where you can be an inspired example of spontaneity.

It is fun to take the deck along on hikes or picnics. During a rest time, you can bring out the deck and let each person choose a "play" card. How each person becomes acquainted with their image or fairy tale is then part of the surprise of the day. Using the cards in nature is especially wonderful and enriching.

Using the cards at bedtime is a beautiful way to end a busy day, for the images of the day are what feed us at night. A special deck could be kept on a child's bedside table or bookshelf, and the choosing of a "dream card" could become a nightly ritual. This could be helpful for a child with evening fears, for the image could be put under her or his pillow as a guardian or protector. Or, you may want to intentionally pull particular cards such as The Guardian Angel, The Fairy Godmother, or Wishing Upon a Star, to be on their bedside table at night.

Holidays and festivals are times to use the deck as well. There are certain cards in the deck that can be brought out to enhance table decorations. For instance, the St. Nicholas card could be placed among the Christmas stockings. The Six of Wands (the Maypole dancers) could be placed next to a vase of freshly cut flowers on May Day to evoke the spirit of springtime, and the Seven of Crystals (the child with the menorah) could be placed near the Chanukah candles. There are many possibilities, including Easter (Mother Goose), the solstices and equinoxes (The Yellow Brick Road), and birthdays. On each birthday, the deck could be brought out, a card selected, and this could be seen as the child's true birthday card.

All of these suggestions are meant to be expounded upon and changed according to your family, friends, and playmates. The true mission is to unite with the cards and let them speak their own language. These examples are intended for children of any age from one to one hundred and beyond! Let the child play within your heart. Enjoy.

Layouts

Before shuffling the cards, choose an appropriate layout for your reading. This is an important step in the process, as the mental choice for the layout immediately "conditions" your subconscious, allowing it to magically select the right cards for particular positions in the layout.

Shuffling the cards is another significant ritual. Each individual has a style in this regard, and we simply suggest that you shuffle with sensitivity and care. Realize that you are putting your vibrations into the cards and that the cards will respond to your deepest longings, desires, and spiritual needs. In some kind of mysterious way, your own subconscious will guide the shuffling and card-selection process. Go with the flow and open yourself to the wonder and joy of your heart's secret realm of wisdom.

When choosing cards from the shuffled deck for most layouts, first fan the cards, always keeping them face down, and then use your left hand to select each one. The right side of your brain controls and guides the left side of your body. Thus, your left hand is more in alignment with your imaginative and intuitive "right brain," while your right hand is more connected to the rational, logical "left brain." However, if you are left-handed, the opposite may be true. When putting the cards into the layout positions, always keep the cards face down until you are ready to read them.

Another of our key recommendations concerns "reversed cards." Many tarot teachers and writers accept the idea that reversed cards mean the opposite or reverse of upright cards. We strongly suggest that you ignore that any cards are reversed and simply make sure each card appears upright. When tarot decks are created, the designers spend many hours preparing beautiful works of art. The suggestion that a reversed card means you should reverse the meaning of the card seems to be a negative use of the deck. Accepting the idea of a reversed meaning gives power to the part of the mind that emphasizes duality, polarity, and division. Furthermore, the process of trying to analyze a reversed card and its message takes you away from the divine guidance flowing to your personality from your subconscious and higher teachers through the pictures in the reading. Every card will speak to you, but only if you are looking at the image the way it was painted and drawn initially.

THE WISHING WELL

After your meditation and shuffling, fan the cards into a circle in a clockwise fashion. This process creates The Wishing Well layout. From this circle pattern, select any card, turn it over, and put it in the center of the well (the circle).

This is an ideal layout when you are looking for one answer to a particular question and when you are truly *wishing* to plumb the depths of your own soul. Realize that the one card you have chosen is a spiritual mirror for your life at this moment. Out of the entire universe of seventy-eight images in *Inner Child Cards*, you have selected this picture as a catalyst for change and inspiration. Consider how extraordinary it is that, for some unknown reason, seventy-seven other cards were not appropriate for you to examine at this time. As when you toss a lucky coin or stone into a seemingly bottomless wishing well, a gift from your heart's secret well of wisdom and love appears—in this case, in the form of the card. Treasure this manifestation of your child within.

This layout can also be done with a group as a special beginning to a meeting or gathering. Each person can shuffle the cards, and everyone in the group can help fan the cards into a circle. Then one individual, chosen by the group, can carefully and sensitively choose the one card that will signify the group's purpose in the days and weeks to come.

Keep in mind that the power and magic of The Wishing Well layout comes from the fact that only one card is chosen to reveal the mysteries of life. In numerology, 1 is the key to unity, wholeness, and spiritual strength.

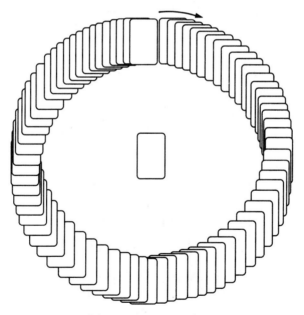

The Wishing Well Layout

WHAT'S AROUND THE CORNER?

This layout is our version of a simple past, present, and future reading containing three cards. The number 3 is always connected with synthesis, creativity, joy, and divine inspiration.

After fanning the cards, select three cards from any-where in the deck to represent the first house (the past), the corner (the present), and the house around the corner (the future), positioning the cards from right to left. Just as a child might be on a bicycle, traveling from his or her home around a corner to a friend's house, you are currently leaving one reality and turning a corner into your next experi-ence. Past, present, and future can all be understood as you "make the turn."

```
              ┌──────────┐
              │          │
              │    1     │
              │          │
              │   PAST   │
              │          │
              │ first house│
              │          │
              └──────────┘

  ┌──────────┐  ┌──────────┐
  │          │  │          │
  │    3     │  │    2     │
  │          │  │          │
  │  FUTURE  │  │ PRESENT  │
  │          │  │          │
  │house around│  │  corner  │
  │ the corner │  │          │
  └──────────┘  └──────────┘
```

What's Around the Corner? Layout

While this layout allows you to create a story in time, it also helps you realize that every action creates a reaction that calls for an eventual resolution. The ancients referred to the trinity as a system of thesis, antithesis, and synthesis. All threefold readings can help you integrate body, mind, and spirit in a rich and revelatory way.

THE CHILD

This is a five-card reading that is filled with wonder and magic. After fanning all the cards, choose five from any-where in the deck and place them face down in a row from left to right. To understand the significance of each place-ment, consider the spiritual meaning of each letter in the word *child*.

Card one is connected with the letter C. This letter begins the word and is shaped like a crescent moon. The card in this first position represents your receptivity to the world around you—your openness to the universal forces shaping your destiny.

Card two is connected with the letter H. This letter looks like a ladder. The card in this second placement in-dicates how you climb higher within yourself to reach a new level of spiritual understanding.

Card three is connected with the letter I. Isn't it amazing to realize that at the center of the word *child* is the letter I, symbolizing individuality, independence, and the I or *ego* developing within? The card in this third placement in the layout signifies a central reality in your life, a special goal, a "change of heart" that can transform your existence.

Card four is connected with the letter L. The card in this position stands for the new *life* you are constantly creating,

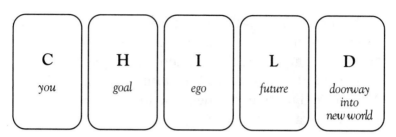

C	H	I	L	D
you	goal	ego	future	doorway into new world

The Child Layout

the *love* you are attracting to yourself and sharing with others, and the *laws* of the world that you must comprehend.

Card five is connected with the letter *D*. In the Hebrew alphabet, D was called *daleth* and was signified by a door. The card in the fifth position of this layout is your doorway into the world and the challenges and opportunities on your immediate horizon. The card appearing in this spot also signifies the "quintessential you," that unique aspect of your life that is often hard to fathom and almost impossible to describe.

It is important to note that, in numerology, the word *child* adds up to 36, which reduces down to 9. CHILD = 3+8+9+(12)+4=36/9. Each letter of the alphabet has a number affiliate based on that letter's position in the twenty-six-numbered sequence. Thus, A=1, H=8, L=12 (can be reduced to 3), X=24 (can be reduced to 6), and so on.

Why should the number 9 be so important relative to child consciousness? This is part of the mystery of life. What we do know is that the human embryo takes nine months to develop during gestation. There are also only nine primary numbers (after 9, the numbers essentially repeat themselves on a higher scale).

As we were preparing this book and contemplating the

significance of *Inner Child Cards* appearing in the early 1990s, we felt there was a special connection between the child within and the number 9. It now appears that this rapport is genuine and that the 1990s are destined to be a crucial decade for healing the inner child and recognizing the needs of children from all over the world. In keeping with this theme, it is highly significant that the planet of healing and the key to the Ageless Wisdom, Chiron, moves through the sign of Leo from 1991 to 1993—for the first time in nearly fifty years. Leo is the main zodiacal sign relating to all aspects of child consciousness.

THE RAINBOW

All layouts using a sevenfold system of cards contain an element of enchantment and mystery. The rainbow of seven colors has always been seen as a covenant between the spiritual worlds and human life. It is a sign of heavenly and earthly magic, and interpenetration.

Fan the cards in the usual fashion and then choose seven cards from anywhere in the deck. Place them into an arc

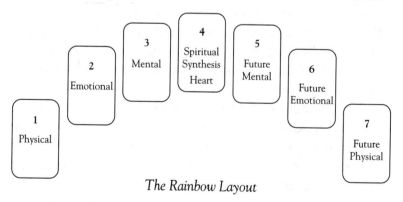

The Rainbow Layout

from left to right, in which the first three cards lead up to the top (fourth) card, and the last three cards follow, completing the pattern.

There are several ways to interpret the cards in this layout. The simplest is to see cards one, two, and three as representing your physical, emotional, and mental development in the recent past. Card four signifies the synthesis of this growth or experience right now, a spiritual shift that needs to be recognized. Cards five, six, and seven symbolize reflections of your future mental, emotional, and physical development. In this method, there are subtle yet important links between cards one and seven, between cards two and six, and between cards three and five—with the fourth card as the unifying heart of the reading.

The seven colors and seven chakras (centers within the etheric body) can also relate to the seven cards in The Rainbow reading. Therefore, the sequence of images in this layout can actually help you understand if a part of your body needs healing or if an aspect of your personality needs nurturing. Very inspiring cards representing a particular chakra may indicate the need for true blossoming in that area. Or, the appearance of a special card relating to a color may be a sign that you should wear clothes with that color more often or perhaps add foods of that color to your diet.

The number 7 is also crucial in terms of soul expression. In some schools of thought, it is said that the soul truly takes control of the physical body at age seven. At that time, the *ego* or I incarnates more fully into the child, allowing the next seven years to be ones primarily devoted to emotional growth (ages eight through fourteen). This is then followed by seven years emphasizing mental expression and development (ages fifteen through twenty-one). Then there are another seven years of spiritual gestation (ages twenty-two through twenty-eight), a cycle often ignored in our Western culture that is focused on materialism and monetary gains.

HOPSCOTCH

One of the earliest games that children love to play is hopscotch. Although there are several varieties of this game, the one we have selected uses ten squares or boxes. Hopscotch is played by tossing a stone into numbered boxes and then hopping or jumping in the boxes to retrieve the stone and return to your original position. To proceed in the game, you have to toss the stone into each numbered box without it touching a line. While hopping to retrieve it, you can't put your foot on a line. The word *scotch* actually means "line." The aim of the game is to be the first child to successfully toss the stone into all ten boxes and hop back to the starting position after you have retrieved the stone from each box.

It is rather striking that hopscotch, with its ten squares, parallels the ten energy centers (Sephiros) in the Tree of Life of the Hebrew Kabbala. The Tree of Life is one of the great mysteries in esoteric philosophy. It is a system or device for understanding and contemplating spiritual existence, life on Earth, and the wonders of human evolution. The Tree of Life is connected with the twenty-two letters of the Hebrew alphabet and the twenty-two Major Trumps of the traditional tarot.

The game of hopscotch, in its own way, is a "tree of life" for a child. It teaches the child discipline, patience, focus, eye-hand coordination, poise, balance, goal orientation, and even rudimentary mathematics. It's one thing for a child to mentally count numbers; it's something else when a child in a group "hops" through the numbers and experiences them in a real game of life.

After fanning the cards, choose ten from anywhere in the deck and place them face down in the numbered boxes of the Hopscotch layout. The meanings for each position are shown in the diagram. These meanings correspond to

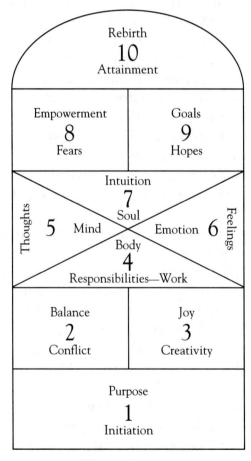

Hopscotch Layout

the major keynotes of the first ten numbers. You can also see that, as in The Rainbow layout, there are unusual interconnections among the numbered placements. One balances ten, two reveals a rapport with nine, and three aligns with eight. In the center of Hopscotch, we experience the four-square world of our central selves—the physical, emotional, mental, and spiritual universe in which we reside. The first three cards can signify our own internal divine trinity, while the final three images can represent the triune synthesis of experiences awaiting us in the external realms.

THE SPIRAL STAIRCASE

Anyone familiar with mystery novels and suspenseful film classics will recognize the form of The Spiral Staircase. But what does it truly represent? In an odd way, it is a reflection of the spiral-shaped DNA molecule that holds the genetic code, that utterly unique internal design that makes a human being completely distinctive. In this regard, it is fascinating to note that the building blocks used by DNA to form human proteins are amino acids, and there are twenty-two primary amino acids actively at work in human cells. This may reveal a formerly unknown connection between the twenty-two Major Trumps of the tarot, the twenty-two letters of the Hebrew alphabet and the twenty-two "building blocks" of the cellular child within.

The Spiral Staircase may also symbolize the serpentine kundalini energy and power that is said to be coiled like a snake at the root chakra in every person, ready to be released and offer enlightenment for an individual during a moment of spiritual initiation. Ultimately, this staircase is the step-by-step unfoldment of our lives on this planet. It can represent the evolution of our reincarnational selves or the year-by-year progress in one single lifetime.

In our version, there are twenty-two steps on The Spiral Staircase. This layout is designed for a reader eager to look at the first twenty-two years of a child's life. Each card signifies one year. Another way to utilize this reading is to break it down into three sevenfold sequences topped by one final card synthesizing the entire reading. In this way, the first seven cards signify the child's physical evolution, the second seven represent his or her emotional growth, and the third seven connect with his or her mental unfoldment. The twenty-second card is the zenith or pinnacle, the spiritual life guiding the seeker on the path.

Because this reading has twenty-two actual placements, its structure carries an enormous power. The number 22 is also connected with 0, (the two numbers delineate the end and beginning of the Major Arcana), the planet Uranus (denoting revolution, change, intuition, breakthroughs), and the ability to build bridges of higher consciousness linking the personality to the soul.

As with the other readings, first fan the cards and then choose twenty-two of them from anywhere in the deck. Or, you could use only the twenty-two Major Trumps in this reading. After mixing and shuffling the cards, place each Major Trump on a step of the staircase. Each card signifies certain experiences or revelations in the first twenty-two years of life. Be sure to keep a record of such a reading, particularly when you are focusing on a newborn baby or a young child needing guidance. You may want to do the The Spiral Staircase with the parents of a child, having each parent select eleven cards for their child, thus creating a balanced and well-integrated session and experience.

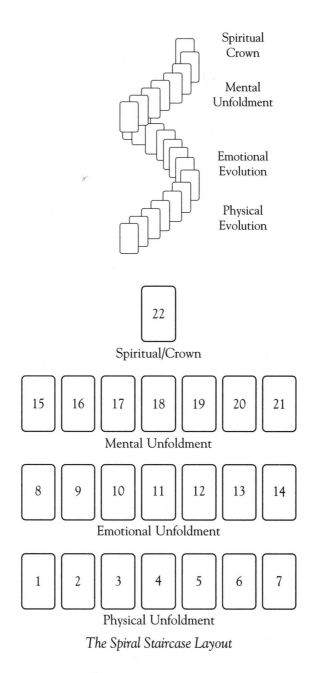

The Spiral Staircase Layout

II
The
Major Arcana

Introduction

As we turn to the twenty-two cards of the Major Arcana, let us synthesize what we have already learned. The system of tarot is a key to unlocking the secrets of the Ageless Wisdom. Each deck that is designed reflects the culture, planetary images, laws, and principles of its times. There are hidden archetypes in humanity's collective unconscious that can be made visible and manifest as a path through the twenty-two Major Trumps or stations of the Royal Road of spiritual existence. One of the most important aspects of being a disciple of higher or esoteric knowledge is the capacity to stay on our own individual paths of destiny. Each one of us has a special purpose in life that unfolds through time. The Major cards, used wisely and inspirationally, help to reveal the meaning of that purpose and the step-by-step process by which it unfolds. *Inner Child Cards* brings to life the magical adventures of the child within and allows us to recover the lost innocence, purity, joy, wonder, and love of the child at heart.

As mentioned, certain fairy tales and children's fables are the archetypes behind the Major Trumps. These tales have a unique way of "telling the story" of the cards. When we focus our attention directly on the Major cards and begin to weave together the images and meanings, several ideas take hold. The Major Arcana is not only a path of human life, it signifies the process of death and rebirth on spiritual levels as well. The Major Arcana reveals the pathway of individual achievements, the lessons in store for us through experiencing intimate relationships and friendships, and the challenges and opportunities that await us when we become dedicated to living a spiritual existence.

A question arises concerning the number of Major Trumps. Why twenty-two? Since we do not know precisely when the tarot originated and who created the system, the following ideas can simply send us in the right direction. When we look at the cosmos and solar system, we recognize eight planets, the Sun and Moon, and twelve signs of the zodiac. Adding all of these together, we note twenty-two celestial influences—one for each of the Major Trumps. Many researchers have linked the pictorial Hebrew alphabet with its twenty-two letters to the Major cards of the tarot. There is definitely a potent connection between these ancient letters and the symbols or archetypes for the twenty-two Major cards.

You may want to investigate two other areas in which the number 22 is dynamically expressed: (1) the book of Revelation, which completes the New Testament of the Bible, has twenty-two distinct chapters; and (2) there are twenty-two different building blocks (amino acids) in the human protein created by the genes of DNA. Thus, the mysterious power of 22 exists in the worlds of astrology, literature, religion, and science. In numerological schools of thought, 22 is considered a "master vibration," a number that acts as a kind of bridge between the human and spiritual realms. That's exactly how the Major Arcana of twenty-two cards functions in an ingenious way.

It is also important to realize that the twenty-two cards represent a circle or spiral of numbers. Try to move away from the archaic Western approach of seeing twenty-two cards or numbers in a linear fashion. Little Red Cap (The

Fool, 0, on the journey of life, God's holy fool, the egg, the circle of wholeness) represents the child within who will experience all twenty-one adventures of human life, concluding with the experience portrayed in the twenty-first card itself, The Earth Child, the child in the cosmic womb awaiting rebirth. While Little Red Cap appears at the beginning of the list and The Earth Child at the end, this is only an illusion. They are joined, and they complete the circle of twenty-two cards. Other students of the tarot, including P.D. Ouspensky, have noted the threefold cycle of seven cards in the Major Trumps with one card (The Fool, 0) remaining. This could refer to the three seven-year periods of growth—ages one to seven (physical), eight to fourteen (emotional), and fifteen to twenty-one (mental)—with age twenty-two being a kind of capstone of the human pyramid, representing the beginning of one's spiritual journey in life.[3]

The following table can be a help in seeing the special connections between and among certain Major Trumps. Keep in mind that there are always numerological links. Cards II, XI, and XX are all connected because of their identification with the quality and essence of the number 2. Cards III, XII, and XXI all have a rapport because of their link with the number 3, and so on. There are other alignments based on the images in the fairy tales. For instance, Little Red Cap, The Big Bad Wolf, and The Three Little Pigs are all associated because of the appearance of the wolf. If two or three of these cards appear in a reading, then the meaning of the wolf must be studied carefully. The Mother Goose and Jack and the Beanstalk cards are connected because of the goose and hen that lay golden eggs. The Fairy

Godmother and Cinderella cards are part of the same fairy tale. You will find many other unusual combinations as you work with the deck.

THE MAJOR ARCANA

No.	Name of Card	Astrological Ruler	Keynote
0	Little Red Cap	Uranus	The Child Within
I	Aladdin and the Magic Lamp	Mercury	The Creative Child
II	The Fairy Godmother	Moon	Wisdom Keeper
III	Mother Goose	Venus	Mother
IV	The Emperor's New Clothes	Aries	Father
V	The Wizard	Taurus	Initiator
VI	Hansel and Gretel	Gemini	Physical Union
VII	Peter Pan	Cancer	Emotional Union
VIII	Beauty and the Beast	Leo	Mental Union
IX	Snow White	Virgo	Spiritual Union
X	Alice in Wonderland	Jupiter	Wheel of Life
XI	The Midas Touch	Libra	Cosmic Balance
XII	Jack and the Beanstalk	Neptune	Sacrifice (making sacred)
XII	Sleeping Beauty	Scorpio	Death/Sleep
XIV	The Guardian Angel	Sagittarius	Protection (High Self)
XV	The Big Bad Wolf	Capricorn	Shadow Self
XVI	Rapunzel	Mars	Purging
XVII	Wishing upon a Star	Aquarius	The Soul Within
XVIII	Cinderella	Pisces	Dreams/Visions
XIX	The Yellow Brick Road	Sun	The Cosmic Self
XX	The Three Little Pigs	Pluto	Call to Rebirth
XXI	The Earth Child	Saturn	Gestating Child

The brief keynotes in the right column are provided to suggest one way of viewing the Major Arcana. Little Red Cap (0) represents the child spirit who will experience various personal and relationship lessons through stages one to nine, culminating in the spiritual union and life of service to humanity of Snow White (IX). This leads to Alice in Wonderland (X) or the spinning wheel of life, karma, ups and downs, the reality of reincarnation. In The Midas Touch (XI) and Jack and the Beanstalk (XII), the child or soul-seeker begins preparations for the sleep known as death in Sleeping Beauty (XIII). Cards XIV through XIX refer to the various spiritual experiences and adventures that the human soul encounters in the afterlife. Then comes the "call to rebirth" or judgment to return to earthly living in The Three Little Pigs (XX). Finally, The Earth Child (XXI) reveals the human soul in embryo, gestating within the solar system's womb, ready and eager to begin a new round of life as The Fool (0, Little Red Cap).

Little Red Cap is also the child spirit who creates a bridge into the Minor Arcana and traditional court cards. If the Major Arcana symbolizes the twenty-two-fold path of human enlightenment, then the fifty-six cards of the Minor Arcana represent the four worlds of life (the physical, emotional, mental, and spiritual) and the attainments or higher levels within those realms (the sixteen court figures). The Little Red Cap card appearing next to any other card in a reading is a reminder to take all the images presented to heart and study them deeply. Hidden within Little Red Cap is the celestial lightning bolt, the sudden awakening, the thunderclap of divine power and illumination.

Little Red Cap

Little Red Cap

The classic fairy tale of "Little Red Cap"—often known as "Little Red Riding Hood"—is a story of childhood innocence, curiosity, excitement at the onset of a journey, temptation, and the primary stages of becoming an individual. Sent to her grandmother's cottage by her mother, Little Red Cap is given a basket of goodies and told to follow the path and avoid the dangers of the woods. As a naive and fearless child, she is curious about the world, open, and has no concept of the dark forces that may be ready to steer her off course and away from her destination.

While traveling the road to Grandmother's house, Little Red Cap meets the Big Bad Wolf and describes her journey to him, ignoring her mother's advice. The wolf encourages her to visit the woods, and she follows his advice and goes off gathering flowers for her grandmother. In the meantime, the wolf goes to the grandmother's cottage, devours the old woman, and lies in wait for Little Red Cap. Near the end of the tale, Little Red Cap enters the house and is also eaten by the wolf, pretending to be the grandmother. As the wolf rests after his meal, a woodsman enters the cottage, cuts open the wolf, and frees Little Red Cap and her grandmother. In effect, they are reborn, and the wolf's stomach is filled with stones, causing him to eventually die. In other versions of the story, Little Red Cap meets the wolf a number of times and learns to outsmart him.

Little Red Cap received her name because the grandmother made her a red velvet cap when she was very young. She loved it so much that she wore it constantly and everyone called her Little Red Cap. As red is a color representing will and fire, the red cap symbolizes the initial stage of spiritual adventure and mental power in the card. In traditional tarot decks, this is The Fool card, often shown by a jester who wears a special cap or hat signifying the presence of divine consciousness.

The wolf lurking in the woods stands for the dark, unintegrated aspect of consciousness and the temptation to stray from one's higher path in life. He signifies the antisocial tendencies within ourselves and reappears in various guises—wicked witch, evil queen, fearful giant—throughout the Major Arcana. In the daughter, mother, and grandmother, we see expressed the ancient triple goddess—maiden, mother, and crone.

In a general way, this card also sums up the entire Major Trumps, because Little Red Cap represents the child spirit within, who is traveling the illumined road of higher consciousness. She is sent by the Earth Mother, destined to be reunited with the Grandmother of Universal Wisdom. On the way, she is tempted by the vagaries of life and learns from her mistakes and failures. The woodsman who allows Little Red Cap and the grandmother to be reborn symbolizes humanity liberating the individual soul and allowing it to join the spiritual hierarchy of the planet.

When this card appears in your reading, be ready for adventure. Open to the vast horizon of the unknown and be willing to take risks. Step beyond the limits set by cultural standards. Temporarily you may feel lost, in the dark, as if emptiness has beckoned you into the void. Enter and be reborn. See life more as a game of chance, an opportunity to play. The experience of The Fool often occurs during times of great inner change. It is as courageous as it is humbling to wear The Fool's mask and walk the road into the unknown. Eventually, through the process of rebirth, your genius and intuition can emerge. Remember to wear bright clothes. Have fun. Let the magic and joy of laughter fill your days. Feel the wonder of life all around you.

Traditional tarot archetype: The Fool
Planetary ruler: Uranus

Aladdin & the Magic Lamp

Aladdin and the Magic Lamp

The story of "Aladdin and the Magic Lamp" describes a child's first adventure into a world of mental empowerment. In the actual tale, Aladdin is sent by a sorcerer into an underground garden to obtain an old lamp. He is given a magic ring to help him on his journey. Aladdin finds the lamp, but he is unable to leave the garden. Accidentally, he rubs the ring and a genie appears, granting him several wishes. Wanting to go home, the boy makes this wish and instantly returns to his mother's house. As the mother takes the lamp to sell it in order to buy food, a larger genie appears as the lamp is rubbed. Thus begins the amazing odyssey of Aladdin, an all-powerful genie, the magic lamp, and a quest for enlightenment on the path of good and evil. By the end of the tale, Aladdin has married a princess and—through cunning and ingenuity—has learned how to defeat the sorcerer, who has attempted to steal the lamp for his own sinister purposes.

Essentially, the magic lamp is a symbol of the illumined mind that is overlighted by a genie, representing the powers of the spiritual world and the "genius" potential in every child. The word *genius* comes from Latin and literally means "to be inhabited by a genie." The magic lamp also suggests the awakening power of a child's imagination. This aspect of the mind becomes the playground of fairy tales, myths, and the languages of ancient cultures. *Imagination* has hidden within it the words *image* and *magi*—the latter word derives from the Old Persian and means "seer" or "wizard."

Aladdin symbolizes every child struggling to learn about the magic of words, wishes, language, and communication with the outside world. Note that the genie, who in the story had been living within the lamp in an "underground" garden, represents the inner manifestation of a child's unconscious life force. By making the genie obey his or her wishes, the child discovers the magical connections between thinking, words, actions, and results.

The genie may also be considered the guardian angel of the childlike, pure mind, a presence that seeks to guide the child to self-mastery and ego-awareness. It is from this awareness that a child learns to perform, create, and manifest outwardly the dictates of the spirit-illumined mind or unconscious (the genie and the lamp). In the card, the boy is looking at the lamp, a sword, a wand, and an altar of crystals, signifying the four elemental forces of nature—water, air, fire, and earth—that he will use as tools to guide him on the path of self-realization. The bookcase behind him suggests the presence of Mercury, the winged messenger of the gods.

When this card appears in your reading, realize that you create your own reality from every thought, word, and action. Rather than thinking analytically, explore your creative genius. Recognize the power of affirmations and the need to protect yourself from negative thoughts in the psychic atmosphere. Remember that "naming" objects and people is a magical art. All names are composed of letters, and each letter carries a numerical and spiritual vibration. The *abracadabras* and *open sesames* of children's stories re-kindle the magic of using words as mantrams of power, or phrases of enchantment. Keep in mind that once the genie is "out of the bottle," some danger of misusing power is always present. However, that danger can be transformed into a great adventure of consciousness and mental expansion. Let the light of innocence and imagination rekindle your passion for learning.

Traditional tarot archetype: The Magician
Planetary ruler: Mercury

The Fairy Godmother

The Fairy Godmother

What the High Priestess was to the traditional tarot, The Fairy Godmother is to *Inner Child Cards*. While not the main character in the original Grimm Brothers' "Cinderella," The Fairy Godmother has played a big part in shaping our inner awareness of magical helpers, due to the Walt Disney adaptation of the story.

In several folk ballads, the Fairy Queen is addressed as "Queen of Heaven." Welsh fairies were known as "the mothers" or "the mother's blessing." Peasants called the fairies "godmothers" or "good ladies." They claimed a fairy could transform a human into an animal or stone and back again. In "Cinderella," this is the kind of enchantment that took place: the animals were turned into human helpers until the enchantment spell broke at midnight. In the original "Cinderella," the hazelnut tree—which bloomed from a branch on Cinderella's true mother's grave—is the reborn mother or magical helper to Cinderella.

The legend of the hazel branch, according to the Brothers Grimm, tells how the Mother of God goes to look for strawberries in the woods to feed the Christ Child. As she bends down, a viper springs out of the grass. The Mother of God flees to a hazelnut tree and hides behind it. The viper creeps away. Since then, hazel branches have been a protection against dangerous creatures. The hazelnut tree stands for the most basic life force that cannot be destroyed. This is the force of protection that can be planted and rooted in every human soul.

We have our high priestess or fairy godmother within us. Where we honor her is in the deepest places of our psyche. She grows into our wisdom as we gain faith in the spirit of our eternal and undeniable protection in the universe. In the ancient tarot, The High Priestess is the mystery teacher, the Papess who holds the key to the gates of our inner sanctuary—our innate wisdom, intuition, and prayerful reverence for all life. In ancient Egypt, she was known as Isis and was connected strongly with the rhythms and cycles of the Moon.

The Fairy Godmother is an enchantress, a holy sacred mother of the ancient mysteries. She ushers in what we think we do not know or cannot have or dare not express. She offers our innate wisdom to believe in—be it miracles or magic or our divine intelligence. She offers us gifts of the spirit: the gifts of inner guidance and universal love.

When this card appears in your reading, your higher mind knows the answer. Listen to your intuition. Cultivate your faith. Be compassionate to the children of the world and those who lack spiritual strength. The number 2 is a balance between the spiritual and physical realms. It is also a balance between the inward way and the external path. Two is an emotional number, and deeply sensitive. Two prominent fairy godmothers—in *The Wizard of Oz* and

"Cinderella"—come in times of need, times of crisis. The Fairy Godmother reminds you of the journey ahead and the need to persevere, to accomplish soul work.

Note: There is an intimate and important link between The Fairy Godmother card (II) and the Cinderella card (XVIII). They are not only part of the same story; the Cinderella card was also traditionally called The Moon, and the Moon is the planetary body associated with The Fairy Godmother card.

Traditional tarot archetype: The High Priestess
Planetary ruler: The Moon

Mother Goose

Mother Goose

A distinct connection exists between the ancient Egyptian mystery of the golden egg and our fairy tale Empress, Mother Goose. Many links can also be found to the Goose that laid the Golden Egg and a great mother from ancient Egypt. Mother Goose has a pointed hat—like that of an Egyptian crown. This story originated in ancient Egypt, where she was Mother Hathor, incarnate in the Nile Goose. She laid the golden egg of the Sun, another way of saying that she gave birth to Ra, the Sun God. The solar disk was sometimes called the goose egg. The Nile Goose was also referred to as the creator of the world, because she produced the whole universe in a primordial world egg.

Venus, the planetary ruler of both the traditional Empress and of Mother Goose, was represented in ancient times as a cow, or the bull from Taurus, the sign Venus rules. Often the goddess Venus was addressed as "The Great Cow Who Gives Birth to the Sun." Orpheus said that the great goddess Darkness, or Mother Night, first brought forth the world egg that was identified as the Moon. This gives a more profound meaning to the children's rhyme "the cow jumped over the Moon."

Mother Goose is a personification of the Earth Mother,

offering the abundance of life to every human soul. The ancient Egyptian symbol for the world egg was the same as for an embryo in a woman's womb. Mother Goose brings us rhyme and riddle, and the musical, humorous, and profound secrets that live within a child's heart. In a sense, she is a "birther" of our essential mental consciousness (the radiant light of the Sun) and our feelings and emotions (the reflected light of the Moon). Mother Goose as The Empress in *Inner Child Cards* offers us unity with the entire world and all the kingdoms of nature. She stimulates our love for flowers, herbs, trees, birds, animals, rocks, precious stones, and the soil itself. When we are one with her, we are one with the life force of the cosmos.

When this card appears in a reading, open yourself to the birth potential within you. The primordial egg is hatching. New life and new beginnings are becoming actualized. Watch your dreams for clues about the future. Feel the abundance of life within your heart. Experience the joy of sensual touch. Let the healing powers of the plant kingdom work their magic within your mind and your etheric or energy body. Realize that each chakra or center within your etheric body is like an egg waiting to crack open and reveal its spiritual splendor. Mother Goose is the provider of a wealth of manifestation. She offers you an egg, wherein lies the whole of your universe.

*Note: Because of the hen laying the golden eggs in the story of "Jack and the Beanstalk," there is a special rapport between Trumps III and XII. In addition, numerologically, the number 12 of this twelfth card of the Major Arcana reduces to the number 3.

Traditional tarot archetype: The Empress
Planetary ruler: Venus

The Emperor's New Clothes

The Emperor's New Clothes

The Emperor is building and constructing (qualities associated with the number 4) based on his desire to attain earthly power. This desire is a component within each of us, and it must be complemented by the creative blessing of The Empress. The harvest of life is actualized in accordance with natural laws—not the political, expedient, and man-made laws belonging to the realm of The Emperor.

A danger is indicated by this card if The Emperor has lost touch with the nurturing presence of Mother Goose (The Empress). It is always the Mother Goddess who brings balance, peace, and beauty to The Emperor on his throne, who represents the power of the material world and the resources accumulated from the four corners of the globe.

When The Emperor becomes greedy, unaware of his surroundings, blind to the folly of his self-centered ways, he becomes a dangerously foolish representation of humanity. The fable "The Emperor's New Clothes" is a primary example of this fool-heartedness. The Emperor or Earth Father is seen without his new clothing—symbolizing the material world—because he has lost touch with reality, thanks to two cunning tailors anxious to swindle great monetary rewards from the Emperor's coffers. A child, with wisdom, a pure heart, and innocence, points to the Emperor and awakens the people to this travesty and embarrassment. The child stands for the unconditional part of the soul that still reveres truth and order in accordance with nature.

When The Emperor is in alignment with The Empress, there is the potential for grounding cosmic power and spirituality of the highest order, for the polar opposites of male and female become harmonized and work in cooperation. Both of these polarities live within each of us. It is in accordance with the divinity of humanity to cherish and honor both polarities. This has not happened for the last two to three thousand years.

It is important to note that The Empress, Mother Goose, precedes The Emperor in The Fool's journey of self-actualization through the Major Arcana. In early Asiatic civilizations, kingship depended on the choices of women. Marriage with the earthly representation of the Goddess, in the form of a queen, was essential to the position of kingship. This was the original meaning of "holy matrimony." An inner marriage with the receptive female energy (number 3, the Earth spiral) is necessary for the ordered male side (number 4, constructive power) to produce law based on wisdom and love in the universe.

When this card appears in your reading, realize that we build upon the past. We move toward the future from the wisdom we have gained. The Empress is the wisdom of life; The Emperor is the application of that wisdom in the attempt to create a better world. The Emperor stands for the limitations of time and the realms of order and mechanical law. He can symbolize blindness, foolish behavior, and self-destructive tendencies, or the sudden awakening to the unity, grace, and spiritual treasures buried within the material world.

*Note: There is a direct connection between the Emperor (IV) and the king in Sleeping Beauty (XIII), who foolishly forgets to invite the thirteenth, or Black, fairy to a party for his daughter. This rapport between the cards is also apparent because number 13 of the Sleeping Beauty card reduces numerologically to 4, the number of The Emperor card.

Traditional tarot archetype: The Emperor
Zodiacal ruler: Aries

The Wizard

The Wizard

In traditional tarot decks, the fifth card of the Major Arcana is known as The Pope, often seen as a rather rigid ruler of the church and a cold figure anchoring Christian teachings on our planet. He possesses the mysterious keys to heaven and Earth. In the twentieth century, some tarot deck designers renamed this figure The Hierophant, connecting this being with the high priests of Egypt and other ancient cultures who were specially and rigorously trained to be initiators for disciples on the spiritual path. Many esoteric writers have pointed to a mysterious hierophant who initiated neophytes in the Great Pyramid thousands of years ago. Plato and even Jesus, in some accounts, are said to have experienced this magical event.

In *Inner Child Cards*, this archetype has become The Wizard, who is not only an initiator and hierophant but a kind, sensitive, and compassionate teacher as well. From our childhoods, we may associate various images with this figure. There is the Wizard of Oz, an imposter who hides behind the curtain. There is the sorcerer in whose chambers Mickey Mouse labors in Walt Disney's *Fantasia*. Then, of course, there is Merlin, guide and spiritual teacher to young King Arthur.

However, the figure who best exemplifies the qualities of the wizard in this deck is the Wizard Gandalf of J.R.R. Tolkien's epic story *The Lord of the Rings*—composed in three volumes entitled *The Fellowship of the Ring*, *The Two Towers*, and *The Return of the King*. This trilogy has thrilled children and adults for several decades now. It is a thoroughly magical and mesmerizing tale that introduces us to the inhabitants of Middle-earth: hobbits, dwarves, elves, ents—tree beings—the Nine Nazgul or Black Riders, the Orc demons, the palantiri (crystal globes or far-seeing stones), serpents, monsters, the Wizard Gandalf, the dark lord Sauron, and so many others. While the entire plot is too long and complex to summarize here, the main story revolves around the need to destroy the One Ring that can insidiously control the owner and that also holds power over other rings devised to keep dwarves, humans, and elves under the spell of Sauron. Frodo, a beloved hobbit, becomes the primary ring-bearer, and he and his many companions join in a fellowship to return the Ring to the shadowland of Mordor, where it can be destroyed, eliminating the malevolent power of the Ring on life in Middle-earth.

Gandalf, with his staff of wisdom, the sword Glamdring, and the horse Shadowfax, plays the part of wizard, magician, spiritual teacher, and guardian to Frodo and the hobbits. He also is the foil and nemesis to Sauron. Gandalf, as an emissary of the divine consciousness overlighting Middle-earth, warns Frodo—representing the child spirit on the journey of life—about the nefarious power contained within the One Ring. He tells Frodo how it can corrupt and entice the wearer, and eventually warp the bearer's personality until it becomes a vehicle for and tool of the dark lord Sauron.

The relationship between Frodo and Gandalf is a clear example of the modern rapport between student and master, child and wise elder. One of the main lessons that Frodo learns is that true spiritual power is not within the One Ring but within the ring of fellowship—one's circle of friends, loved ones, and companions on the path of life. Thus, *The Lord of the Rings* speaks of the higher meaning of "group consciousness" and the beauty of community life in what could be a New Age on the horizon for humanity.

When this card appears in your reading, a spiritual teacher is on the scene. Who is inspiring you at this time? Is there a new field of study to explore? See the realms of music, art, literature, philosophy, religion, history, and nature as pathways to higher knowledge. Build a bridge between the child within that seeks answers and the Higher Self that continually offers jewels of enlightenment through dreams, visions, promptings, and intuitive flashes. When breakthroughs occur and inspirations flood your mind, be willing and eager to share your newfound wisdom. Avoid the temptation to rigorously hold on to revelations. Steer clear of controlling others for your own purposes. Most of all, with your visualization skills (based on the development of your third eye, or *ajna* center), see your life linked with a fellowship of like-minded souls, your true ring of power in the world.

Traditional tarot archetype: The Hierophant
Zodiacal ruler: Taurus

Hansel & Gretel

Hansel and Gretel

In the traditional tarot, this card has always been depicted as The Lovers. It conveys the need for trust and loyalty in committed relationships. On a higher level, it symbolizes the balance between physical and spiritual love. The story of "Hansel and Gretel" allows us to see a rudimentary form of divine love at work in the adventure of dedicated siblings, a brother and sister.

In the story, a poor woodcutter lives with his wife and two children. The wife is the children's stepmother, and she is very cruel to them. In order to survive, because they have very little food, the stepmother coaxes the husband into abandoning the children in a forest. This reveals his weak willpower and her selfish desires. The children are brought to the woods—the unknown, the pathless world—and left to fend for themselves. The moonlight (receptive, feminine, higher wisdom) plays a significant role in guiding Hansel and Gretel. They are also guided by two white birds. First, a dove leads them to a candy house (personal desire, cravings, oral fixation, material security, beginning awareness of sexuality). Next, a white duck helps them cross the water (emotional security), acting as a bridge to bring them to a new level of love and awareness.

Hansel and Gretel need to work together in harmony, to trust each other implicitly. In finding the candy house, they believe they have found heaven since they have been suffering so long without food. Hansel nibbles at the roof (head, spirit) and Gretel nibbles at the window (soul). They are well fed and fattened up, and the witch who lives there ushers them to tiny beds. When they awaken, they realize they are prisoners.

In religious writings, the dove often appears as an image of the Holy Spirit. In fairy tales, the pure spiritual forces, as yet untainted by the senses, are also symbolized by the dove or another white bird. The old crippled witch, symbolizing the intellect, is blind to the true nature and growth of the eternal in the human being. Ultimately, self-destruction occurs when she attempts to outwit little Gretel. It is the young girl who instead tricks the witch, pushing her headlong into the fires of her own large oven. The witch, who had wanted to devour the children, signifies the dark regions of consciousness that must be recognized and purified in the fire.

At this point, the children are liberated. Gretel (the soul) has rescued Hansel (the spirit). United, brother and sister return to their home. However, in order to arrive safely at their parents' house, they must enter a new state of consciousness. The earthly soil is no longer capable of supporting them. They must travel across water, the stream of flowing life, on the wings of spirit (the white duck). On the highest level, once spirit escapes from the snare of the sense world (the candy house, carnal love), it begins to recall the true home from which it sprang (eternal love).

When this card appears in your reading, a deep spiritual initiation or union may be taking place. Realize that each person has a feminine/masculine balance and that it is now time for you to bring these inner components into a state of balance and equilibrium. Hansel is a symbol of the animus—the wind, the spirit, and male energy. Gretel signifies the anima—the soul, nurturing, and female energy. Together, hand in hand, their rapport indicates a preliminary form of the divine marriage. Meditate on the beauty of these two children inspiring each other, and remember that they reflect the lost love of their parents, who have been worn down by the rigors of life. The spiritual embrace, the romantic touch, the heart-centered gaze can allow you to reexperience the richness and wonders of the world.

Traditional tarot archetype: The Lovers
Zodiacal ruler: Gemini

Peter Pan

Peter Pan

A ship is often depicted in mythological or spiritual teachings as a vehicle of the soul, moving consciousness from one shore to the next. In the fairy tale "Peter Pan," Wendy and her brothers not only learn to fly—freeing themselves from the physical limitations of time and space—but they also land on an island and encounter a great ship where Captain Hook rules. Captain Hook and his band of pirates symbolize the chaotic elements of the underworld, our untamed fears. Tinkerbell is the elemental spirit within us, the fairy deva. She is a light body and can produce spells for good or evil depending on the calling of the heart. Wendy and her brothers represent humanity. They are tethered to the poles and roots of their incarnation, yet by *believing* in other worlds, they manifest the ability to soar beyond the boundaries of time.

Traditionally, the seventh Major Trump is known as The Chariot. This mechanical device is seen as a symbol for the body, which carries the mind and spirit. The charioteer stands for the inner self, and the horses represent the divine willpower that must be harnessed. This card calls for balance between the Earth-centered life and the life of spirit. When individuals are in touch with their inner guides, they know not to control the guidance but to move gracefully according to their environment—open, free to explore, and reveling in the spiral dance of day and night, the balance of light and dark.

In the story of "Peter Pan," this archetypal pattern is at work. The children are tempted to stay in never-never land forever, becoming eternal children like Peter Pan, and never reaching the maturation stage of the human soul. But the children are symbolic of the part of us that must return to the center, finding our way back home after having experienced all of life's adventures. In a sense, Peter Pan is like the two horses of the chariot, symbolizing the elemental will that moves us beyond, pulling us forever forward into our adventures, untamed and unbridled. Ultimately, the quest of our journey is to find our santuary and soul heritage. The chariot, Peter Pan, Tinkerbell, and the great ship are all guiding and illuminating facets of our cosmic self.

Another idea needs to be remembered here. As we encounter obstacles and sudden twists and turns on the road ahead, we must not *pan-ic*, a term supposedly engendered by the cry of the great god of wild nature, Pan.

Because the comet/planetoid Chiron was only discovered in 1977, it has not yet achieved a position within the twenty-two-fold system of the Major Arcana. However, a likely place for it would be here, in alignment with The Chariot and Peter Pan. Chiron begins with the *ch* of *chariot* and *child*. Peter Pan signifies the child who always stays young at heart.

As this book was written, Chiron had been traveling in the sign Cancer for the first time in nearly fifty years. Cancer is the zodiacal sign traditionally associated with this card. Chiron is often associated with the key that opens doorways to higher consciousness, the qualities of the maverick, the wounded healer, and the Ageless Wisdom teachings. The soaring joy of Peter Pan and the flickering light of Tinkerbell are associated with the positive qualities of Chiron, while the darker presence of Captain Hook seems to be aligned with the Chirotic wounds of the past that are difficult to heal. It is also interesting in this regard to remember that the captain has a hook in place of a hand and that the Greek root meaning of *chiro* is "hand."

When this card appears in your reading, move steadily in life and uncover your secret resources. Ride the middle path, a road that eventually turns around completely and takes you home. While it makes sense to strive for safety and security on a day-to-day basis, allow yourself the freedom to dream, fantasize, and be adventuresome. Take a canoe trip, sail into the sunset, or listen to the pounding of the waves against the shore. Spend a few days in the wilderness and watch birds take flight, warble their songs, and feed their young. Let yourself fly into exalted realms of imagination. If you believe you can, you will.

Traditional tarot archetype: The Chariot
Zodiacal ruler: Cancer

Beauty & the Beast

Beauty
and the Beast

In the original version of this classic fairy tale, Beauty lives with her father, two sisters, and three brothers. She is noted for her kindness and sensitivity, while her sisters are greedy. The family is very rich, but the father has a boat-wreck and loses their wealth. Beauty works in the fields and is very humble. The father hears that his treasures may have been found, so he ventures on a long journey, but just before departing he asks his daughters what they would like. The two sisters want valuable jewels and clothing; Beauty asks only for a black rose. The rose is the star of life in the realm of flowers, and black represents the *unseen* beauty within, the hidden beauty of the rose, the hidden beauty of humanity.

The father leaves but does not recover his lost fortune. Instead, he arrives at a castle. All the doors are open, the fire is roaring, and food is laid out. He eats, rests, and spends the night. The next morning, he gets up and visits the garden, where he plucks a rose. Suddenly, the Beast, a man with the head of a lion—symbolizing the black rose or hidden beauty—appears in the garden. He gets angry and says he will forgive the father if he can have his daughter. The father receives riches from the Beast.

Beauty visits the Beast at the castle. She sees his kindness, and she continues to watch him. The castle is beautiful, and she has splendid feasts. One day, she finds a tower and sees a mirror. The mirror says, "Through time—in your heart—you will see the truth."

Beauty begins to have a recurring dream in which she is at a lake and meets a handsome prince. An old crone tells her that she needs to learn about spiritual beauty, and the compassion in her heart keeps growing for the Beast.

One day Beauty's father becomes ill and she goes to visit him. The Beast asks her to return within three weeks, saying, "I'll die without you." She stays longer than the allotted time and then looks into a mirror and sees the Beast dying by a lake. In that moment, she realizes that she loves the Beast. She rushes back to the castle and finds the lake, takes the Beast's head in her arms, and says she loves him. Her tears flow on him and as he stirs, she goes to get a drink. Then she sees the prince from her dream, reflected in the lake. When she turns around, the Beast has been transformed into a handsome prince.

The prince tells Beauty that an ugly woman once came to his castle, and he treated her poorly. She cursed him by turning him into a beast and indicated that the spell would only be broken when someone could see his true inner beauty. It was Beauty who was able to break the enchantment with her unconditional and genuine love.

The story of "Beauty and the Beast" is an inspirational fable that generates music in the heart. The age-old lesson or moral is that beauty is in the eye of the beholder. In the traditional tarot, this card is called Strength and often pictures a beautiful woman opening the mouth of a lion! When this card appears in your reading, accept the miraculous gift of love in your life, not for what you can visibly see, but for what you feel and know as truth. True love is available to us when we open our spirits to inner guides and dreams, and dare to follow our hearts. Love is often disguised, as is truth. Look beyond the mask, beyond the personality world, and beyond the surface and stereotypes. Where there is darkness, see light, Where there is pain, send healing prayers and thoughts. Where there is disharmony, sow seeds of contentment and joy. Let your warmth and magnanimity be expressed to loved ones, friends, the greater community, and humanity as a whole. When you look in the soul mirror, be thankful for the beautiful gift of divine life and eternal love.

Traditional tarot archetype: Strength
Zodiacal ruler: Leo

Snow White

Snow White

Hidden within the fairy tale of "Snow White and the Seven Dwarves" is a major lesson concerning service to humanity and the utilization of wise discrimination.

Just before Snow White is born, her mother is sewing and pricks herself with a needle. As the blood flows, she wishes for a child with lips as red as blood, skin as white as snow, and hair as black as ebony. Snow White soon comes into the world, but her mother dies during the birth.

Snow White's stepmother is a beautiful but wicked, vain, and jealous queen. When she asks the magic mirror—symbolizing the search for perfect beauty (an aspect of the sign Virgo, which rules this card)—who is the fairest in the land, the mirror replies, "Snow White." The queen is so angry that she then orders a huntsman to kill Snow White and bring back her heart as proof of the deed. The huntsman—representing humanity, mortality, and humility—has compassion for the young girl, lets her go, and brings back the heart of a young animal for the stepmother.

Snow White, at seven years of age, is alone in the forest, seeking shelter and protection. She is on a symbolic wisdom pilgrimage. She finds a small cottage with seven beds and seven bowls—the number seven signifying a major spiritual transition. When the dwarves find her, after working all day in the diamond mines, she is fast asleep in one of their beds. In the original version of the story, the dwarves are gnomes. The gnomes represent earthly wisdom, the inner light shining from within the depths of our planet. Snow White begins to grow into her higher wisdom by taking care of the gnomes–cleaning their house and making meals for them.

The wicked queen finds out that Snow White is still alive by asking the magic mirror again who is the fairest in the land. Over many years, this stepmother tries to kill Snow White three more times. The first time, disguised as a merchant selling lace, the queen gives some material to Snow White, who pulls it too tight around her waist. She faints—due to a restriction of her breathing (spirit)—and is found by the gnomes, who revive her. In the second encounter, the stepmother transforms herself into a woman selling combs. Snow White is tricked again and buys one—poisoning her head and scalp (ego identity). The gnomes rescue her once again. In the third experience, the stepmother changes herself into an old woman selling apples that she has secretly poisoned. Snow White, still lacking in wise discrimination, takes a bite of a poisoned apple and appears to fall dead. Actually, she falls into a deep coma from which the gnomes cannot revive her.

The earthly wisdom has run its course, and Snow White is ready for her final initiation. She cannot stay in the cottage (darkness) forever, so the gnomes place her in a glass coffin where the light streaming through the forest can illuminate her body, heart, and soul. She needs to come *into the light*. Her inner service—dutiful work for the gnomes, cleaning, nurturing others, being humble—has been completed. The prince comes. He picks her up, takes her to his horse, and, as he carries her, the piece of poisoned apple is dislodged from her throat. This is a symbolic clearing of the throat chakra and a reempowerment of Snow White's primal wisdom. United with her *animus* (the prince), she has become crowned (seventh chakra) in wholeness and light.

Traditionally, this card in the Major Arcana is known as The Hermit and is often portrayed as a wise old man or woman (crone). Through the pilgrimage and odyssey of Snow White, we learn about becoming whole when all the aspects of the soul life and personality life are fused and integrated. Living in an isolated or separate state will not bring happiness and contentment. The active work we are called to do in life is only partially physical, emotional, and mental. There is also our soul work, our service to humanity, the opportunity and challenge to be a "light to the world."

When this card appears in your reading, you may be at a critical point in your journey toward spiritual enlightenment. Reflect on your recent travels, studies, and interpersonal experiences. Be discriminating in your choice of business associates and personal companions. Let your earthly life mirror your soul's longing to be of service to humanity and all the kingdoms of nature. Banish those aspects of yourself that are petty, vindictive, and harmful to others. Allow your words, heartfelt love, and understanding to form an inner radiant light that can heal friends, relatives, and the greater community.

Traditional tarot archetype: The Hermit
Zodiacal ruler: Virgo

Alice in Wonderland

Alice
in
Wonderland

When the beloved children's story *Alice in Wonderland* begins, Alice is sitting next to her sister on a hot summer's day by a riverbank. Later, when her epic adventures in the realm of dreams and kaleidoscopic visions are over, she returns to exactly the same spot by the river's edge. Her psychic journey with the White Rabbit, the March Hare, Tweedledum and Tweedledee, the Mouse and the Caterpillar, the Cheshire Cat, figures shaped like cards led by the Queen of Hearts, and other bizarre characters has been a complete cycle, a spiral dance of the mind, a circular odyssey. Everything about *Alice in Wonderland* brings us back to the image for the tenth card of the Major Arcana, The Wheel of Fortune.

Children have always adored merry-go-rounds, Ferris wheels, and magical spinning wheels of all kinds. The ancient Wheel of Fortune is a symbol of the numerous experiences (ups and downs) of a lifetime, the wheel of many lives, the spiritual reality of reincarnation. Coming after The Hermit card, which signifies humanitarian service and illumination to the world, The Wheel of Fortune suggests the need to prepare oneself for a future incarnation and the greater spiritual life ahead.

Two characters—at the start and end of *Alice in Wonderland*—particularly stress the higher keynotes of this card. The White Rabbit who leads Alice into Wonderland pulls a watch out of his pocket and keeps saying that he is late for an important date. This emphasizes the keynote of *time*, the great cycle of minutes, hours, days, months, and years—the wheels upon wheels of duration that appear to fill eternity. The outer clock has become suspended as Alice falls down the rabbit hole into another dimension of time.

Later on, the strange figure of the Queen of Hearts keeps saying, "Off with her head!" It seems that the thinking and intellectual aspects of the brain must be put on hold at this stage of reality. One must somehow become a true Queen of Hearts and penetrate to the center of life where the pulse of life is strongest. Ironically, by the story's close, Alice, on the verge of reawakening, sees the entire pack of cards from her dream rising up in the air and falling upon her. It is fascinating to note that the Alice in Wonderland card is midway—at the center—of the journey through the Major Arcana and that Alice's cards are surrounding her.

A larger theme of Alice in Wonderland is that all of life can be likened to a dream. Plato, Shakespeare, and other authors have pointed us in this direction, and Lewis Carroll (in real life, a tutor of mathematics and librarian named Charles Dodgson) created his adventures for Alice Liddell, an English child, in 1864. Carroll loved the world of games and enjoyed inventing novel approaches for the imaginative amusement of children. The constant play on words in the story is extraordinarily profound and reveals the circuitous logic and playfulness in language.

When this card appears in your reading, see your life from a higher perspective. Explore the realm of dreams and keep a notebook of your out-of-body journeys. Good fortune may be just around the corner. Anticipate a turning of the wheel of fortune in your favor. Be the eternal optimist. Know that the power of prosperity consciousness is your ace in the hole. Take advantage of golden opportunities coming your way. Good luck is on your side. Let it ride!

Traditional tarot archetype: The Wheel of Fortune
Planetary ruler: Jupiter

The Midas Touch

The Midas Touch

Throughout the evolution of the tarot, this card has usually been portrayed as a female figure, sometimes blindfolded, representing cosmic justice. Sitting upon a throne, holding a sword of spiritual power in her right hand and the scales of divine justice in her left hand, this goddess of wisdom was known as Themis in ancient Greece and Maät in ancient Egypt. As one moved toward the afterlife, there was a need to "balance one's accounts" and be weighed in the celestial scales as a human soul. The children's story of "The Midas Touch" is a profound teaching on this subject.

In the tale, King Midas has a beautiful daughter whom he loves very much, but closer to his heart is his desire for gold. One day, while he is counting his wealth, a stranger appears and asks him what he would like more than anything in the world. The king, without forethought, abruptly asks that everything he touch become gold. The mysterious stranger tells him that by sunrise the next day his wish will be granted. As the first rays of light enter the king's chambers in the morning, the king is astounded to see that his wish has indeed been granted. A chair, his bed, and even the glorious roses in his garden turn to gold at his very touch. However, his daughter, who loved the roses, runs to her father terribly upset at this sudden turn of events. The king reaches out to comfort her, and, shockingly, she turns to gold as well.

Beside himself with grief, the king once again encounters the stranger, who asks the mighty ruler if he has learned his lesson. King Midas begs that the golden touch be taken away. The stranger tells him to dive into a pool of water in the garden with a special vase and fill it with water from the depths of the pool. This represents a ritualistic cleansing of his sins of avarice and pride. Midas is told that if he pours this water on everything that has been turned to gold, all his precious objects will once again be restored to their natural state. Sure enough, the stranger's words hold true and King Midas is able to bring his daughter and the beautiful roses of the garden back to life.

The clear moral of this fairy tale is that there is something much more precious and close to our hearts than material wealth or gold: the beauty and sacredness of life all around us. Another lesson is to think ahead concerning the implications of your acts, for your innermost wishes may very well come true, causing more grief than happiness.

When this card appears in your reading, be sensitive and loving to the people around you and turn your back on greed. Appreciate the simple and beautiful things in life by realizing that all that glitters is not gold. The gentle touch of a loved one may be more important than making money or struggling to earn a promotion. Balance out your life.

Trust your intuitive judgment over cold logic. Weigh your decisions carefully to avoid harming yourself and the people you love.

Traditional tarot archetype: Justice
Zodiacal ruler: Libra

Jack & the Beanstalk

Jack
and the
Beanstalk

The ancient images for The Hanged Man, the twelfth card of the Major Arcana, almost always reveal a person suspended on a cross of living wood—a figure upside down with arms crossed. This individual is linked to various myths concerning the dying savior, the messiah who comes from heaven to liberate humanity. It is someone reversing his or her view of life, symbolizing the need for self-sacrifice and spiritual at-onement.

In the fairy tale "Jack and the Beanstalk," a young boy, caring for his poor mother (representing unfulfilled earthly abundance) after the death of his father, climbs to another world (the sky) to discover new riches for the human soul. In this drama, Jack's mother asks him to sell their last cow for food and provisions, but Jack buys some magic beans instead and brings them home. His mother feels the beans are worthless and tosses them into the garden. However, while she weeps over their sorry state, Jack looks out and sees that a mighty beanstalk has grown up over night, rising beyond the clouds. Jack climbs the beanstalk several times, visiting a strange castle in the sky inhabited by a giant and his wife. Ultimately, Jack is able to seize a hen that lays golden eggs, bags of money, and a magical harp that plays itself. In the final act, the giant chases Jack down the beanstalk, but the young lad is able to chop it down, causing the giant to fall to Earth and be killed. It is Jack's daring and ingenuity that bring prosperity and abundance back to his family. In other versions of the story, the giant killed Jack's father originally and took the family's wealth and sacred possessions.

The Hanged Man must reverse his view of life in order to surrender to the new birth of awareness that faces him in the next stage on the path (Death, XIII). Jack needs to go to another, higher realm to "reverse his fortune." He cannot depend on the physical reality that lies before him. By daring to explore a new dimension of consciousness, he is able to bring a fountain of inexhaustible riches into the world.

The issue of surrender is strong in this card. Jack surrenders the cow in order to purchase the magic beans. The buying of the magic beans signifies that Jack can no longer remain attached to the world of logic. In a way, he is betting that a magical new life can begin from the sprouting seeds. His mother also experiences a ritualistic surrender by giving up all hope and tossing the beans into the garden. Her crying is like an emotional release, a liberation of all her suppressed hurts and fears. It, too, is a magical act that changes the future of their lives.

Every human soul carries heavy burdens, and the beanstalk linking heaven and Earth symbolizes the cross that we must bear. Part of our lesson is learning that we can vanquish the giant, who personifies the phobias, fears of the unknown, and monsters of hate, greed, and anger that lurk in the shadowy regions of our psyche.

When this card appears in your reading, see your life and primary relationships from a fresh perspective. Meditate for clarity. Improve your posture and realize that your spine is like a spiritual beanstalk that carries divine impulses up and down your body. Realize that you can conquer giant problems with just a little bit of enlightenment. You can change your world through the power of positive thinking and the ability to visualize yourself steeped in abundance. Turn over a new leaf. Go with the flow. Surrender to your spiritual destiny.

Traditional tarot archetype: The Hanged Man
Planetary ruler: Neptune

Sleeping Beauty

Sleeping Beauty

In the tale "Sleeping Beauty," a daughter is born to a king and queen, and invitations to a celebration are sent to lords and ladies and all the fairies. At the celebration, twelve fairies arrive and begin offering a variety of wishes, but one fairy—the thirteenth, called the Black Fairy—has been accidentally forgotten, her invitation lost. This fairy bursts upon the scene and curses the child, saying she will die when she pricks her finger on a spindle. This horrifies the king, queen, and attendees; however, one last good fairy has not made her wish. She cannot remove the Black Fairy's curse completely, but she is able to alter it so that the child will only sleep for one hundred years upon pricking her finger.

To prevent the curse from harming his daughter, the king orders all spindles to be destroyed. But one day, when the young girl is in her teens, she enters an old attic room in a high tower where she finds the Black Fairy weaving on her loom. It doesn't take long for the curse to take hold when the young girl pricks herself on the golden spindle. Instantly, she and everyone in the kingdom fall into a deep sleep lasting one hundred years. At the end of that time, a young knight, brandishing a sword, cuts through the thicket of trees that had grown up around the castle. He enters the building and finds everyone asleep. He comes upon the young Sleeping Beauty and with one kiss on her forehead, breaks the evil spell, awakening her and the dormant kingdom. At long last, the family is reunited, and there is much rejoicing in the land.

The story of Sleeping Beauty suggests the long process of maturation, particularly that point in the cycle when an innocent girl enters the strange world of adolescence, begins to menstruate (represented by Beauty pricking her finger on a spindle), and then awaits the relationship that will carry her to a new life of marriage, family, and worldly responsibilities. In the sleeping part of the tale, there is an emphasis on receptivity, the quiet interlude of several years when nothing momentous seems to occur externally for a young person but deep changes happen internally to the child in the forms of sexual and emotional transformation. While the adolescent period for girls is symbolized by the monthly blood flow of menstruation and their growth into young women, for boys it is symbolized by the deepening of their voices, signifying a greater strength and ability to express themselves in the world.

This "change of life" or transfiguration for a child is a process of death and rebirth. In the story, the thirteenth fairy curses the daughter with death. This card, the Death card, is also number 13. However, this death curse is quickly altered into a sleep of one hundred years. Death and sleep are immediately intertwined within the plot. We learn that death never kills the soul or divine spark of life within the human being. Death is a long sleep from which we will awaken, eventually to be reunited with loved ones. The one-hundred-year period is an evolutionary cycle roughly equivalent to a time period during which a human soul might be disincarnate, a time period of learning on inner levels before returning to the earthly world. Even in Greek mythology, sleep and death—*hypnos* and *thanatos*—were considered "brothers." We know that every evening of sleep is like a miniature death, a chance to die to yesterday's triumphs and failures and to rest up before tomorrow's opportunities and challenges. The knight on horseback in this card offers the "kiss of consciousness" to Sleeping Beauty in the form of stardust. He represents the active aspect of Sleeping Beauty's higher existence, the force in touch with her celestial nature.

Ultimately, the soul can be seen as the true Sleeping Beauty. It sleeps until the balance of feminine and masculine creates a divine marriage of heaven and Earth, spirit and matter. When reincarnation and cosmic evolution are accepted by humanity, death will cease to hold its terror for us and will, instead, be seen as a long sleep, an interval of time when we can steep ourselves in the wisdom gleaned from the grand adventures on this planet.

When this card appears in your reading, a long period of contemplation may be needed. Do not be afraid of the quiet growth occurring within. Enter the world of dreams, archetypes, and symbols with courage and emotional calm. Learn while you are in a receptive state. *Doing something* externally is not always an answer. Let go of the past. Like the caterpillar changing into a butterfly, a magical process is underway in the depths of your being. Eventually, you will sprout wings and soar like an eagle over formerly uncharted realms of knowledge.

The process of metamorphosis is dangerous, but every child must go through this incubation period before becoming an adult. The young person must leave the safety net of childhood, but the joys and sorrows of that time span will live on in the imagination.

This card also suggests the healing power of sleep. Without enough rest, the cells of the body cannot function properly and the immune system is stretched to its limit. See the peace and quiet of sleep as an interlude of tranquility and recuperation. During sleep, the soul loosens its grip on the physical body and roams the spiritual universe (while still maintaining its tie to the body through the "silver cord" or thread of consciousness). Enjoy this nightly excursion into another realm of existence and bring back the fruits of those experiences in the forms of amazing dreams, visions, and plans for the future.

Traditional tarot archetype: Death
Zodiacal ruler: Scorpio

The Guardian Angel

The Guardian Angel

Over the centuries, the fourteenth card of the Major Arcana has been depicted as an angel or archangel, often pouring a magical elixir from one cup to another and standing with one foot on solid ground and the other foot in a pool of water. Known as Temperance, this figure represents the unification of spirit and soul energies, and on another turn of the spiral, it represents the alchemical process by which a human personality becomes infused with divine light and wisdom. In *Inner Child Cards*, the image on this card is The Guardian Angel, the being who watches over the evolution of a child and protects and heals it during times of crisis.

In the Middle Ages, the great painters of Europe drew halos above the heads of angels. This was the cosmic sign that these beings were ringed in spiritual light and were emissaries of God. Later on, saints, priestesses, magicians, and other celestial messengers (the literal meaning of the word *angel*) were also shown overlighted by a halo. Thus, divine glorification and initiation do occur within the human realm. Guardian angels are seen either as forces outside ourselves keeping us from danger, or as soul aspects of our identities, or even as our Higher Selves. While part of the meaning of Temperance is moderation and abstinence, the word's higher association is with the Latin *tempor*, a time period or season for all things under heaven. There is also a link to the Latin *temperare*, meaning "to mix, blend, or regulate." Aleister Crowley, in designing his tarot deck, called this card Art. To create beautiful art or music, one combines the angelic or higher forces of inspiration with physical materials and instruments. This is reminiscent of the age-old fascination with alchemy, the changing of lead into gold, where lead is the unenlightened personality and gold is the soul-infused spiritual disciple.

In esoteric circles focusing on meditation, visualization, and magical rituals, there is a special goal that is often described as the attainment of conversation or communion with one's holy guardian angel. Apparently, all human beings are blessed with angelic presences who nurture and guide us during incarnation, but we each have an overlighting figure, who might be termed our Good Angel, watching over us. We merge into this angel when crossing the threshold known as death. More and more people are discussing their revelatory experiences, which often include life-transforming encounters with a guardian angel or exalted light being. In children's stories, fairy godmothers, helpful wizards, and good fairies are variations on the greater theme of The Guardian Angel.

When this card appears in your reading, open your heart and mind to the gentle rhythms that can restore your sense of balance and equilibrium. Often when we are making major life changes, we need protection and guidance. As a young child, it is very important to feel safe. The Christian prayer calling on the guardian angel has brought peace to many children: "Angel of God, my guardian dear, to whom God's love commits me here, ever this day be at my side to light and guard, to rule and guide." In much the same way, as adults we have learned to surround ourselves with white light when in danger or doubt. Do you feel safe and secure? Call for the assistance of higher forces. They will come and tenderly embrace you.

Traditional tarot archetype: Temperance
Zodiacal ruler: Sagittarius

The Big Bad Wolf

The Big Bad Wolf

In the tarot, the fifteenth card of the Major Arcana is usually called The Devil. Artists have drawn this figure either as a batlike creature with enormous wings or as a demonic image with horns who has chained a man and woman to his throne—a cube, symbolizing the four-square material world. In *Inner Child Cards*, the traditional Devil card is replaced with The Big Bad Wolf.

The wolf appears in many children's stories, particularly "Little Red Cap," "The Three Little Pigs," and "Peter and the Wolf." He is usually the personification of negativity, badness, darkness, and that which attempts to devour us and take away our lives. (*Evil* is *live* backwards, and *Devil* is the reversal of *lived*.) The fox is another variation of the Big Bad Wolf appearing in many nursery rhymes; in the Uncle Remus tales, he is Brer Fox. It is remarkable to note that the numerical value of *fox* is 666, the so-called number of the Beast from Revelation at the close of the New Testament.

On a psychological level, fairy tales tell us important truths about the darker and shadowy sides of life. These truths do not necessarily point to a world of evil but reveal the struggles of the human ego as it seeks balance and understanding in the physical universe. The more one strenuously and righteously strives to avoid the dark side, the more destructive the shadow life may become. As one accepts the presence of the shadow and the mysteries of Creation, the light within ourselves begins to grow. In the dark or ugly side of human nature lies the seed of true spiritual integration.

The Big Bad Wolf and the sly fox personify the cunning, harmful, and mischievous side of the human intellect. Ultimately, it cannot remain dominant, because it is programmed for self-destruction. This is revealed by the wolf in "Little Red Cap" and "The Three Little Pigs," the witch in "Hansel and Gretel," the evil queen in "Snow White," and the giant in "Jack and the Beanstalk." When The Devil card appears in a reading from a traditional tarot deck, it seems to carry a threatening tone because its message holds reminders of hell, shame, and sin. The Big Bad Wolf is a far more natural expression of the devilish forces within us, signifying the subconscious shadow of the mind and the collective darkness (unenlightened consciousness) within humanity.

Healing comes to the human soul when it accepts and merges darkness with light. When we honor our wholeness—including the haunting thoughts, the imagined shame, the seemingly unpardonable sins—then we are no longer victims of our fears. We become spiritual students and initiates of the higher path of cosmic evolution.

The drawing of this card is important. The wolf is hiding behind a tree in a barren forest. Fertility and growth have disappeared. The Tower—symbolizing the coming purging of ego attachment, lust, and desire—lies in the distance. The spiritual path to higher goals still exists, but the road seems desolate and shadows are numerous. The wolf will have to stop hiding and venture forth into the moonlight to be healed. This represents the movement out of bondage to self-centeredness and into communion with the world at large.

When this card appears in your reading, embrace the fears, doubts, and unintegrated aspects of your psyche with open arms. Let your light shine into the darker regions of your mind. Accept yourself as a blending of higher and lower selves, a union of spiritual and material bodies. Call up your anger, jealousies, and antipathies, and transfigure them into joy, compassion, and understanding. Where there is separation, sow harmony and togetherness. Where there is pain from mental anguish, offer heartfelt sensitivity and simple acts of kindness to friends and relatives. Reverse the pattern of lying to yourself and others. Learn to speak and live out the truth of your existence to the best of your ability.

Traditional tarot archetype: The Devil
Zodiacal ruler: Capricorn

Rapunzel

Rapunzel

The lightning-struck tower has always been the central image for the sixteenth card of the Major Arcana. Over the centuries, it has been designed with male and female figures falling from the top of the tower walls. This symbol portrays the purging of ego-centered consciousness and the recognition that material foundations cannot be the basis for spiritual life. Humanity can erect a Tower of Babel, elegant buildings, and shimmering skyscrapers, but humility must accompany our greatest efforts and achievements as we reach toward the heavens. The fairy tale "Rapunzel" represents The Tower in *Inner Child Cards*.

In the story, a couple prays for a child. The woman's wish is granted and while she is pregnant, she sees a beautiful garden over her fence. She asks her husband to take some of the greenery that grows there. However, it turns out that this garden belongs to an enchantress, and the husband is caught stealing herbs. The enchantress tells him that in order to live he must promise her his daughter. Hastily, he agrees, abandoning common sense for the love of his wife.

The daughter is named Rapunzel, and at age twelve (the onset of puberty) she is taken away by the enchantress. She is locked into a tower that has no steps. Besides her beauty, she has a wonderful singing voice and a long, golden braid. Rapunzel has never seen a man other than her father. One day, a prince traveling in the woods hears her sing and watches as the enchantress calls, "Rapunzel! Rapunzel! Let down your hair." Rapunzel drops her hair from the tower window and the enchantress climbs up her braid. When the enchantress leaves, the prince calls for the braid and ascends to the top of the tower. Rapunzel is frightened at first, but then soothed by his gentle voice and sensitive manner.

The enchantress finds out that Rapunzel has been visited by the prince, cuts off her braid, and abandons the young girl in a desert. When the prince returns, the enchantress takes Rapunzel's place in the tower, puts the braid down, and, as he climbs up, cuts the braid, causing the prince to fall into brambles and lose his sight. While wandering around blind, he meets Rapunzel in the desert. Her tears of joy heal his vision, and they live happily ever after together with their twin children, a boy and a girl.

Traditionally, this card has been affiliated with the planet Mars. The fairy tale focuses on ego-oriented issues. Hair is a manifestation of ego. Rapunzel is unevolved, yet in the tower she goes through deep changes. This is symbolic of the fact that we cannot enter the tower until we reach puberty. Then we are moved beyond ourselves, shocked into new awareness. Rapunzel's singing represents the awakening of her throat chakra, emphasizing her need to be heard and recognized by the world. Her long hair is connected with the unfoldment of ego-centered consciousness.

In Rapunzel's situation, her new life is the desert experience where she gives birth, symbolizing her initiation into a greater existence. The blinded prince symbolizes the need to stop our active pursuits and to avoid becoming dependent on our outer senses. Each individual at The Tower stage of reality must journey within and cultivate her or his higher psychic abilities and intuitive thought processes. When this card appears in your reading, be prepared for transformative experiences. The only certainty now is change and metamorphosis. Unexpected and shocking events may be on the horizon. Purge your ego of old desires, fears, and grudges. A sudden mental breakthrough can help release you from personality attachments and limitations. If you are working as an artist, musician, builder, designer, or in any fine craft, take a new look at your materials. Allow your physical tools and resources to reflect the light and love radiating from spiritual levels of consciousness. In social and relationship matters, let your hair down for a change of pace.

Traditional tarot archetype: The Tower
Planetary ruler: Mars

Wishing Upon a Star

Wishing
Upon a Star

On the highest level, the previous four cards in the Major Arcana tell the story of the human soul as it crosses over the threshold of death into the afterlife (XIII), merges with the Guardian Angel (XIV), encounters the Dark Angel (XV), and ultimately purges and releases itself from old karma in The Tower (XVI). This leads to The Star experience in the seventeenth card and the rekindling of divine light, wisdom, and radiant love. In *Inner Child Cards*, this card is called Wishing Upon a Star.

The ancients regarded stars as living entities, sometimes heavenly angels. Jewish scriptures maintain that "every affair in which a person is engaged here on Earth is first indicated up above by the angel of their star." This reminds us of the adage attributed to Hermes Trismegistus: "As above, so below"—what's true in the macrocosm (solar system) is true or reflected in the microcosm (the human being).

To wish upon a star is to connect once again with the higher forces of life, be they guardian angels or celestial bodies of light. The star of the cosmos is mirrored on Earth as the five-pointed star seen through an apple core or a five-petaled flower such as the rose. The five-pointed star is also a symbol for the creative aspect of humanity and the evolutionary potential of each individual. Making a wish followed by an offering to a wishing well is a form of prayer and ritual that goes back many centuries. The association with water reveals the enchanting power of water goddesses and the Moon.

All of us wish for our dreams to come true. As children, these wishes are often in the form of fantasies and imagination: "I wish I could fly"; "I wish I were a fairy princess"; "I wish I were a ballerina"; "I want to be a fireman when I grow up." The urge to wish is magical. It brings us in touch with a potential not yet actualized, a vision, a hope. To wish is to open ourselves to receiving, and if we believe ourselves to be worthy of fulfillment, most likely our dreams will be realized in one form or another.

The saying "Be careful what you wish for" is an important caution. As children turn into young adults, wishing must become more of a conscious act. Many people are not aware of the power of wishing or of the guardian star-presences who overlight them. Remember that it is a sacred act to wish upon a star, a calling to the Great Mother and Father, the bearers of celestial gifts for each one of us.

When this card appears in your reading, an important wish, desire, or hope may be fulfilled soon. Open your mind and heart to your star-self, your higher identity that guides you upward on the path of destiny. You may want to go out in the evening or just before dawn and commune with the heavens, attuning yourself to the magnificent presence of a planet ("wandering star") like Venus, Mars, or Jupiter, or a brilliant first-magnitude star such as Antares, Sirius, Aldebaran, Regulus, or Arcturus. Remember that your true essence is spiritual light, clothed in this life by a physical body. Your exalted prayers and thoughts have the power to uplift and heal friends, loved ones, and your greater community.

Traditional tarot archetype: The Star
Zodiacal ruler: Aquarius

Cinderella

Cinderella

The human soul that has liberated itself from the past and freed itself from earthly attachments must continue on its stellar odyssey. The final four cards of the Major Arcana weave a story concerning the great dreams of humanity (in traditional tarot, The Moon, XVIII), the alignment with the divine source (The Sun, XIX), the call to rebirth in human form (Judgment, XX), and the gestation into a new cycle of earthly evolution (The World, XXI).

The eighteenth card of the Major Trumps has always been associated with the sign Pisces. Cinderella is given, by turns, wooden shoes and glass slippers to wear, and Pisces rules the feet or the "understanding" part of the body. She is also continually cleaning up the home and being a slave to her stepmother and stepsisters, displaying the Piscean themes of self-sacrifice and martyrdom. On a higher level, Cinderella also attends the Magical Ball, which symbolizes a child's wonder of growing up and becoming part of the large society, and meets her dream prince (Pisces rules dreams). The Moon card suggests the vivid power of imagination, fantasy, and deep-seated feelings; it also signifies the astral realm surrounding the Earth, the dimension of consciousness containing all of humanity's longings and desires.

In the original fairy tale, Cinderella is the daughter of a rich man. Her beloved mother dies and her father remarries a woman with two jealous and petty daughters. Since the father is often away and the stepmother takes charge of the home, Cinderella is removed from her high standing and becomes a maid; she sleeps in the kitchen and is given wooden shoes to wear. One day, Cinderella's father is about to go on a journey, and he asks his daughters what they would like. The stepsisters ask for jewels and valuable gifts, while Cinderella requests only the first branch that touches her father's head on his return trip by horseback. Upon his return, her father brings Cinderella a hazelnut branch, which the young girl plants on her mother's grave. The hazelnut symbolically refers to protection: it represents the spiritual thread that cannot be destroyed by the powers of ignorance and darkness.

As the years pass, the hazelnut branch grows into a beautiful tree that is filled with birds from all over the world. The branch symbolizes the life force that links Cinderella to her origins, her mother, the Kabbala, the Tree of Life, and her spirit (the birds). As she cries at her mother's grave every day, Cinderella waters the tree and, in so doing, shares her deepest sorrow and feelings with her mother. Astrologically, feelings, origins, and the mother are connected to the Moon.

The prince of the land announces that there will be three balls to attend. To keep Cinderella from going, the wicked stepmother gives her difficult tasks that require hours of hard work. Also, she is given no dresses to wear to the balls. Cinderella, overwhelmed and exhausted, runs to the grave and cries. Suddenly, the birds, who are her angelic helpers, bring her a magnificent dress and glass slippers to wear. In essence, these are a treasury of gifts offered to Cinderella by her mother and the Tree of Life. Cinderella is thus able to attend the balls, where she dances with the prince.

At midnight, during one of the balls, Cinderella dashes away from her prince but leaves behind one of her glass slippers. The prince searches his entire kingdom for the one girl whose foot will fit into this slipper. When it is Cinderella's turn to try on the slipper, it fits perfectly, and the beautiful girl and the prince get married and live happily ever after. The wonderful ending of the story reminds us that the soul (Cinderella) and the spirit (the prince) are always a pair whose reunion is a cosmic truth when earthly living has run its course.

When this card appears in your reading, explore your deep feelings about the past, home, the mother, life's mysteries, and the wisdom of Hecate, the ancient Moon Goddess. Recognize the importance of mourning and humility, for they are often stepping stones into a profound joy and radiance of the heart. Ultimately, the most difficult tasks in a lifetime are the result of the spirit at work, strengthening our souls for future service on a broader scale. Reflect. Let tears flow if they must, for they are the waters of life. It is not the outer, physical mother who is the invincible protector for a child, but the healed mother or woman within, who emerges once the soul is cleansed and purified. Perhaps a walk in the moonlight will begin this process of emotional and psychic transformation.

Traditional tarot archetype: The Moon
Zodiacal ruler: Pisces

The Yellow Brick Road

The
Yellow
Brick Road

The nineteenth card of the Major Arcana usually displays a brilliant yellow Sun, revealing the magnificence of this source of life on our planet. In ancient cultures, the Sun was often revered as God and the radiant spiritual presence that makes all things possible. But it was also known that the Sun, shining forth in all its majesty, could destroy earthly life and blind the foolish who stared too long in its direction. In some versions of this tarot card, a little child is shown dancing near a garden of sunflowers or playfully riding a horse. This child reminds us that to attain our divinity we must become childlike—innocent, carefree, and joyful—and that child consciousness will lead humanity out of darkness and into light. In *Inner Child Cards*, the Yellow Brick Road stands for the path to higher wisdom and spiritual truth.

When we reach for the light of the Sun, we are striving to pursue our lofty goals and to gain insight and understanding. In the classic story "The Wizard of Oz," Dorothy and her dog Toto set off on the Yellow Brick Road to find the wonderful Wizard of Oz, who will help Dorothy find a way to return home. The Yellow Brick Road represents the golden path that leads a child onward to Oz—the Higher Self, adulthood, larger society, one's true spiritual home in the solar system, and the Sun. There is even a connection between Cinderella (The Moon) with her glass slippers and Dorothy on her Yellow Brick Road with the magical shoes that she can click three times to bring her back to Kansas.

Along the path, Dorothy meets other seekers—the Straw Man, the Tin Man, and the Cowardly Lion—who accompany her on the journey to self-actualization. The good fairies, evil witches, happy munchkins, and deceitful wizard in this tale are all manifestations of various states of consciousness the pilgrim encounters throughout a life-time's adventures. Nevertheless, the foundation of the story is the Yellow Brick Road, which must be followed to reach the final destination: home—symbolic of the soul awakening, spiritual light, and wisdom.

In primeval times, human beings were said to shine a golden light like that of the Sun; Earth was still impregnated with solar life. This was the Golden Age, when humans walked with the gods and goddesses. Now, in our civilization, only a reflection of this higher radiance can be brought into our everyday lives, but many individuals are relearning how to merge the Sun self with earthly consciousness.

In ancient China, the sage Lao Tzu spoke of the Tao. This Tao was the Way of Life, the path of spiritual destiny. To step off this path was easy, and the way was filled with challenges and upheavals. But to remain centered, bal-anced, and focused on one's divine path was the hallmark of the true disciple and initiate. Now we know from the latest space explorations that the Sun itself radiates a solar wind, a kind of stellar carpet of charged particles and perhaps mysterious healing vibrations that reaches all the way to the Earth. The human soul that lifts its vision higher and higher eventually returns to the core of the Sun to be replenished with divine substance, the manna of heaven. Then, following the golden stream—the Yellow Brick Road—in outer space, the soul can find itself preparing for another earthly incarnation once the trumpet of rebirth is sounded.

When this card appears in your reading, a burst of spiritual sunshine can enlighten your mind and warm your heart. Fill the dark caverns of your psyche with the white light of divine wisdom. Create a rainbow bridge of compassion and understanding over which you can travel to meet with your fellow pilgrims on the path of life. Rise before dawn, walk to a nearby nature sanctuary, and reexperience the wonder of the day's rebirth. Visit the ocean and absorb the splendor of the rising or setting Sun with its orangereddish glow in the western sky. Light a candle, meditate in an aura of peace, and send your healing thoughts and prayers out to humanity on a multicolored beam. Realize that you, no matter what your flaws and challenges may be, are a light to the world.

Traditional tarot archetype: The Sun
Planetary ruler: The Sun

The Three Little Pigs

The
Three
Little Pigs

In many tarot decks, the twentieth Trump of the Major Arcana reveals the Archangel Gabriel blowing his trumpet while a man, woman, and child arise from their coffins. It is a card of spiritual rebirth and Judgment Day, with the real judgment being the decision of the human soul to depart from the higher realms and return to earthly life. On another level, this card looks at the wisdom and discrimination needed to outfox potential enemies and remain centered on the spiritual path. The fable "The Three Little Pigs" describes a final encounter with the Big Bad Wolf, and demonstrates that the powers of evolution eventually triumph over the forces of darkness.

Although some versions of "The Three Little Pigs" portray the clever fox as the pigs' adversary, the widely accepted story centers around a ravenous wolf who sets out to devour his prey. Each pig builds a house that symbolizes a certain type of character and quality of life. The first pig creates a house of straw. The second pig makes a house of furze or gorse, while the third pig builds a brick home. With great ease, the wolf is able to huff and puff and blow down the dwellings made by the first two pigs. Luckily, they have escaped to the third pig's house. But when the wolf encounters the brick home belonging to the remaining pig, he finds he is unable to blow the house down.

The wolf then tries to trick the third pig in three ways. First, he invites the pig to fetch turnips. Next, he asks him to go apple picking. Finally, he requests the pig to join him at a country fair. In all these episodes, the pig learns to outwit his enemy. He goes out an hour earlier than planned to harvest turnips. When picking apples from a tree, he tosses a few away from the wolf, who chases after them while the pig escapes. And while at the fair, the pig buys a butter churn, sees the wolf, hides inside the churn, and rolls down the hill to his home, with the wolf in hot pursuit.

By this time, the wolf is so angry and hungry for the last pig that he decides to climb on the roof and sneak in through the chimney. The wise little pig, hearing footsteps above him, places a kettle with boiling hot water in the fireplace. When the wolf descends, he is scalded to death, and it is the pig who devours the wolf for his tasty dinner.

The success of the third pig in the fable reminds us that the powers of selfishness, greed, and hate—symbolized by the wolf—will eventually be transformed through a fiery purging and cleansing. The triple confrontation between the pigs—who represent aspiring humanity—and the wolf—who represents the potent forces of evil and chaos in the world—reveal a glimpse of the often invisible but true battle between light and dark on this struggling planet in the cosmos.

Ever since its discovery in 1930, Pluto has been given

the rulership of this card. It is a sign that, hidden within the Three Little Pigs' adventure, is an epic tale of death and rebirth, metamorphosis, and victory of the human spirit against great odds. The powerful breath of the wolf represents the spiritual and natural life energies that often wreak havoc around the globe in the form of thunderstorms, hurricanes, and typhoons. When humanity learns to build a strong and sensible foundation for itself on Earth—symbolized by the third pig's brick house—the negative winds emanating from the realm of nature, or the wolf—prove weak and ineffective.

When this card appears in your reading, remember to build the world around you in a practical manner. Is your spiritual, mental, emotional, and physical universe anchored in truth and wisdom? Focus more on quality than quantity while creating beautiful works of art. Follow the call of the wild and listen to the voice within that guides you to fulfill your higher destiny. Take time to make weighty decisions. Realize the implications of your acts for the future. Stop wasting your strength by criticizing others. Recall the ancient adage "Judge not, lest you be judged." Reinforce your positive, upbeat, and inherently good nature so that the dark elements of the world cannot break down your resolve and dedication.

Traditional tarot archetype: Judgment
Planetary ruler: Pluto

The Earth Child

The
Earth Child

In the traditional tarot, this card is The World; in *Inner Child Cards*, it is The Earth Child, an enwombed human soul preparing for rebirth. This child represents the culmination of a long journey. As the soul progresses through the passage of time, space, matter, and spirit, there is a reemergence back into the primordial egg. At birth, a new being, complete and whole, makes its dramatic entrance into the physical world of earth, water, air, and light. This card suggests the potential of future development and the creative interpenetration of multidimensional consciousness.

To be born into the material universe is to experience pain and suffering—ironically, the most common bond uniting every human being on Earth. Appropriately, this card has always been ruled by Saturn, the beautiful ringed planet that signifies discipline, responsibility, concentration, hard work, vulnerability, and the resolution of "old karma." The Tibetan master D.K., writing through his disciple Alice Bailey, confirmed a profound link between Saturn and the Earth. Both planetary bodies are intimately associated with the divine "ray" or force carrying the energy of active intelligence and adaptability.

By learning difficult lessons on Earth, lifetime after life-time, the human soul begins to comprehend the vast scope of existence in the infinite universe. The human embryo itself, while gestating in the womb for forty weeks of preg-nancy, recapitulates the entire evolution of life on this planet as it progressively resembles first reptilian, then am-phibian, and finally, mammalian forms before birth takes place. The beauty, majesty, complexity, and uniqueness of life on Earth are woven together within the fabric of the human baby about to be born.

There is an unusual yet distinct connection between this twenty-first card of the Major Trumps and its numerical reverse, the twelfth card, Jack and the Beanstalk. The bean-stalk that Jack climbs, linking heaven and Earth, is simi-lar to the umbilical cord uniting mother and child. Jack, as a fairy-tale version of The Hanged Man, voluntarily decides to "bear his cross" and move through a process of self-sacrifice. The embryonic soul in The Earth Child makes a spiritually conscious choice to reenter the physical world and once again "take up the cross" of earthly living. Just as The Hanged Man (XII) reverses his understanding to prepare for the transition known as Death (XIII), The Earth Child (XXI) gives up its divine state of bliss to serve humanity and await the transition known as birth (The Fool, 0).

The sequence of twenty-two major cards reaches its culmination in The Earth Child, but this natural process is a circular dance rather than a series of linear images and experiences. The embryo—containing all the meaningful experiences gained in the passage through the Major

Trumps—matures into The Fool—Little Red Cap—and the cycle of life begins anew. For this reason, The Earth Child card is deeply associated with the magic of organic growth and the spiritual forces at work in the "seed state."

When this card appears in your reading, powerful and divine influences are gestating within your aura. Embrace them with an open mind. Remember how protected and nurtured you are by invisible helpers, guides, and teachers. You are never alone. Experience the universal harmony emanating from the Sun, the sacred nucleus of the solar system, and become the rhythmic beating of your own heart—the radiant center of your body. The ancient saying "As above, so below" is true, for cosmic wisdom is encoded in your DNA and cells. Most of all, let a sense of childlike wonder fill your life. See with new eyes. Touch the world as if for the first time. Summon courage for the rites of initiation that lie ahead.

Traditional tarot archetype: The World
Planetary ruler: Saturn

III
The
Minor Arcana

Introduction

While the twenty-two cards of the Major Arcana symbolize the great journey of the human soul on its path of destiny, the fifty-six cards of the Minor Arcana represent the various experiences of the human being within the four worlds of life on planet Earth. The number 4 symbolizes the anchoring of the divine plan on Earth, the manifestation of spiritual laws in reality, the building of solid foundations, and the hard work needed to achieve tangible results. The four worlds are associated with the four seasons, the four cardinal points of the compass, the four elements—fire, air, water, and earth—and the four sacred letters of the Hebrew name of God—the Tetragrammaton. In *Inner Child Cards*, the four suits are signified by Magic Wands, Swords of Truth, Winged Hearts, and Earth Crystals.

The images within the Minor Arcana of *Inner Child Cards* are an evolutionary step beyond the pictures in the tarot decks of the past six hundred years. Often, the traditional Minor suits have been simply represented by, for example, seven swords, five cups, or ten wands on a card, with no scenes, stories, or sensitive messages. In other decks, the drawings show adult figures adorned with many esoteric emblems that are difficult to decipher. In *Inner Child Cards*, the old shepherd's or peasant's staff has blossomed into the Magic Wand, representing the fire element. The medieval metallic weapon of soldiers has been transfigured into an adaptable Sword of Truth that takes many forms, representing the air element. The chalice or Holy Grail of Christianity has been universalized as the Winged

Heart, representing the water element. And the ancient occult pentacle of spiritual fire, which eventually became synonymous with coins or monetary disks, has metamorphosed into a beautiful Earth Crystal, representing the earth element.

Inner Child Cards reveals sensitive, heartwarming, and spiritual scenes throughout the four suits. The fairies pictured in the Magic Wands are the invisible beings who give life and color to the world of nature. The children on diverse adventures in the Swords of Truth express the curiosity of the human soul and the eagerness to penetrate life's mysteries. The mermaids and mermen in the Winged Hearts pull our imaginations into the undersea realm of human emotion and in-depth feelings. The gnomes in the Earth Crystals are the hidden workers who give life and solidity to the land, rocky soil, and mountain ranges that grace our planet.

Each suit has ten numbered cards and four court figures. As mentioned in the section entitled "Introduction," the archaic court figures have been renamed to reflect the spiritual culture of our times. The Page is now the Child, the Knight has become the Seeker, the Queen is the Guide, and the King is the Guardian. The names, images, and qualities for the "court" of *Inner Child Cards* remind us that no matter what path or "suit" of life we follow, there are teachers and exemplars who can lift us into an exalted state of con-sciousness.

During a reading, the appearance of many cards from one suit is an obvious signal to explore the entire range of meaning concealed within that realm. For instance, many wands suggest the need for greater passion and fiery expression in life; many swords reveal a need to take action in the world and seek clarity; many hearts ask one to plunge into the hidden regions of human love and emotional sensitivity; and many crystals point one toward building a better world for oneself, one's loved ones, and the greater community.

While the twenty-two Major Trumps may signify ultimate turning points and milestones in life, the fifty-six Minor cards are by no means "minor" in significance. Use your intuition carefully as these images appear. Free associate to link the pictures with recent experiences in your life or the life of the one for whom you are doing the reading. Think and talk about what you actually see happening in the card. This process may allow you to suddenly comprehend exactly what the card means for yourself or another and why it has appeared at this time.

The Magic Wands

The Magic Wands of *Inner Child Cards* are in accordance with the fire suit in traditional tarot called the wands, rods, or clubs. They symbolize art, creativity, intuition, and all that is magical within the elemental realm of Nature.

Magical divination wands have been crafted for centuries out of tree bark and twigs from various fruit trees and other plants in order to duplicate the creative properties of Mother Earth and her receptive feminine nature. Throughout this suit, a variety of flower fairies and nature spirits celebrate the union of human consciousness with high-vibrational clairvoyance from the devic, or angelic, kingdom. According to Alice Bailey in *A Treatise on Cosmic Fire*, devas see sound and hear color, while humans reverse this process.

The wands open us to joy and passion. They beckon us to go beyond the limits of our human boundaries. The Magic Wands are topped with a butterfly to further imply the natural wonder inherent in the invisible process of metamorphosis. In each of us, this creative transformation can occur metaphorically, again and again, throughout our lifetime.

Ace of Wands

Ace of Wands

In this card, a magnificent soul potential in the form of a butterfly is being unveiled by two fairies. In Welsh mythology, fairies were known as "the mothers" or "the helpers." These fairies are liberating the spiritual quality of humanity. There is a connection between the soul and the butterfly in Greek mythology. This stems from the belief that the human soul becomes a butterfly while searching for a new incarnation. The process of transformation is extremely powerful in our lives as we search for a broad understanding of the future and a gentle surrender to the past. As we emerge from old wounds, we take on new colors and wear new wings of hope—much like the butterfly miraculously unspiraling from the dark cocoon. This butterfly is released into the light and is offered new conscious awareness. This may very well be happening in your life right now.

The butterfly is an essential emblem of love, suggesting, in China, a wedding of souls. This winged gift is a reminder to you today that love, soul unity, and art are fluttering into your life. An inspired rebirth is taking place. It is time to reveal your true colors. The flight has begun.

Two of Wands

Two of Wands

There is a universal belief that one's reflection is a vital part of one's soul. It is said that reflective surfaces are soul catchers or doorways to the world of spirit. Buddhists accept that all existence is like a reflection in a mirror.

Depicted in this card is a beautiful fairy seeking the deeper meaning of her existence. Unlike Narcissus, whose soul was trapped in his water reflection because of his vanity, this fairy is uniting with her "beloved self," or the aspect of her ego that is all loving. She sees in her own image the potential of sacred beauty.

When we are ready for inner transformation, we come face-to-face with our true selves. Who is your true self? Are you radiant and glowing? This is a time of profound personal awareness and insight. Find a place of solitude and serenity and explore your hidden talents. Intuitive gifts strengthen you. Perhaps you can visualize your true face. As one Buddhist koan asks, "What does your original face look like?"

Three of Wands

Three of Wands

The three fairies in this card celebrate the muse of the Triple Goddess. The first goddess was said to be Mnemosyne, or memory, which is the sacred gift in us that offers the ability to recite prose, song, rhyme, and riddle. The three muses provide clairvoyant insight and intuitive skills. From these divine creators come the words *music* and *amusement*.

The fairies pictured in this card play delicate violins. Such beautiful stringed instruments were said to have been made to echo the ecstasy of creation. The fairies play their instruments with magic wands that have been transformed into bows, accentuating the divinity of their play. They are among peach tree branches, from which magic wands were made in ancient China. The peach tree is associated with the planet Venus and represents art, music, and love.

The precious gift to you today is the memory of the muse in your heart. Open to the joy of artistic expression. The music of the universe is constant and flowing. The keynote here is the potentiality of joy—your joy and the joy of life.

Four of Wands

Four of Wands

One of the ultimate mysteries of Creation is the life force contained within a seed. When planting a garden, we prepare the soil much like we would create a cozy bed for a child. We cover the seed with rich soil in order to allow it a period of gestation. Soon, it blossoms into a triumphant plant, bursting forth above the ground and reaching upward toward the sky. The metaphor of the seed is applicable to every aspect of our lives: the seed of knowledge, the seed of truth, the germination of consciousness, and so on.

This card depicts the planting of new wisdom and the reconstruction of an intuitive foundation. The garden has four corners, representing the four seasons and the four cardinal directions. In ancient Greece, the symbols of the seasons were four women: Summer was adorned with a crown of grain; Autumn wore a basket of fruit; Spring wore a wreath of flowers; Winter was bareheaded. The fairies pictured in this card represent springtime, when new planting takes place and a new season of Sun and sprouting awaits.

In your life, new ideas are seeding themselves. Prepare your life for the fruits that you will bear. Plant your creativity and watch it grow.

Five of Wands

Five of Wands

The Roman goddess Flora is an essential figure in nature. She represents all that flowers and blooms, and her festival is May Day. She holds the mystical power of procreation and self-fertilization. One might say she is the queen of flowers.

A five-pointed flower is often called by alchemists "the sacred womb," where all perfection and beauty may arise. Flora, who is pictured in this card as a flower fairy, is honoring the blossoming time that is a vital part of the symphony of nature. She calls upon you to expand and unfurl the divinity sleeping within your heart. Your female side is flourishing. This is an opportune time to paint or color a mandala. Visualize it as the opening of your soul. Realize that this time in your life is not a struggle, but a dance or unfolding of your creative and intuitive gifts. Some changes may be on the horizon. Focus on the constructive freedom the universe is offering you. The keynote is to open yourself.

Consider the significance of this beautiful saying: "And the day came when the risk to remain tight in a bud was more painful than the risk it took to blossom."

Six of Wands

Six of Wands

May Day marks the time of year when the Earth is adorned in her green cloak that is beautifully accented with the flowers of springtime. The presiding deity of this season is the goddess Flora, also known as The Maiden. A Maypole was traditionally set up the evening before May Day. The significance of the Maypole dance was to honor the fertile season of spring. The dance, which spiraled around the pole with ribbons and flowers, was an acknowledgment of the sacred womb of humanity. It was seen as an ultimate gratitude to Mother Nature.

Old rituals like the Maypole dance, Japanese tea ceremonies, Chanukah, and Saint Nicholas day have become trivialized in Western culture. These rites of passage or "holy times" are meant to be harbingers of unity and to strengthen the well-being of the community. They also serve to expand global consciousness and cross-cultural awareness.

The fairy maidens in this card are bringing forth their song and dance to usher in not only spring, but the fertility of their creative powers. They are honoring the apex of a jubilant new consciousness that is blossoming before them. This is a time to express your passionate side and realize that you are a vital part of the continually moving circle of life.

Seven of Wands

Seven of Wands

This is a healing card. The child fairy depicted on the card holds the knowledge of flower healing and the right use of plant remedies to aid in human development and consciousness. The vibrations of the flower devas and nature spirits are so high that their impact and presence are often overlooked by human beings. They offer us the elixir of their flowers through healing agents such as the Bach Flower remedies. These remedies were created by Dr. Edward Bach, who dedicated his life to researching and perfecting the system of flower healing. Dr. Bach said that the flower remedies are "like beautiful music or any glorious uplifting thing which gives us inspiration, to raise our very natures, and bring us nearer to our souls and by that very act to bring us peace and relieve our sufferings."[4]

The seven differently colored butterflies on this card represent the chakra system in the human body. It is an ancient tantric belief that each human body contains seven of these mystic "lotus centers" and that they are located at various levels along the spinal column. Through meditation and deep breathing, we can awaken the kundalini, or life force, which brings health to body, mind, and spirit.

You may be ready to explore the depth and transformation available through chakra healing, flower remedies, or any form of high-vibrational body attunement. A walk in nature could be beneficial. There you can open to the elemental healers who surround and protect our planet. As you heal your own body, you can learn to become a radiant healer for your friends and loved ones.

Eight of Wands

Eight of Wands

Of the four elements, fire is the lightest because it rises upward in the air. Fire moves in many shapes and forms and is used in ritual and ceremony to accentuate transformation, purification, and spiritual awakening. Fire gods and goddesses were said to be born in the woods, much like Greek heroes and heroines were said to be born of tree maidens. These gods and goddesses were then impregnated by lightning and the Sun.

On the Eight of Wands card are eight fairies who are being initiated or reborn into the fiery realm of power and transmutation. Their wands are being reenergized and alchemized as they invoke the birth of new consciousness. Ultimately, what is truly being awakened in them is the light of the world.

Join these fairies as they light their wands in the blazing fire. It may be time for you to reunite with a group, family, or consciousness that moves you beyond self-interest or personal power. The way you use your power has significant consequences in the world. Fire can destroy or heal. Become a light bearer who honors truth and feels compassion for all who share the Earth.

Nine of Wands

Nine of Wands

There are times in life when we are shown the gateway to new awareness that is beyond our current boundaries or resistance. This new awareness offers another view of the world that can recapture, or open us to, the magical garden of wisdom that lives within us. It is there that we may learn to master our abilities and gifts.

When the fairy on this card is ready to open the garden gate, she will discover a world of herbs, flowers, and trees that await her arrival. They will revitalize and heal her. There is an abundance of energy available to her. The butterflies on the gatepost are the aspects of her soul that are ready for metamorphosis. She hears the garden calling, and so she peeks.

This is a wondrous time in your life when you may be exploring the secret passages of your spirit or completing an important evolutionary cycle. There is a rich and flowering place within you. You must journey there. Close your eyes and envision yourself entering the colorful and fragrant gardens of your mind and heart.

Ten of Wands

Ten of Wands

Once the decision is made to cross the threshold into a magical garden, the long journey toward rebirth reaches its destination. The fairy who was gazing into the garden in the Nine of Wands is now entering and experiencing a spiritual homecoming in the Ten of Wands. The multicolored butterflies on the gate have been transformed into a crown of white butterflies, creating a divine aura of protection and guidance. The fairy holds in her hand the magic wand, tipped with a beautiful rainbow butterfly, symbolizing her initiation into states of higher consciousness.

The number 9 in numerology often suggests completion, while the qualities inherent in 10 are rejuvenation and exaltation. With nine white butterflies encircling her and the tenth now a part of her magic wand, this fairy is ready for new responsibilities and service in the intuitive arts: healing, art, music, dance, and ritual.

While meditating on this card, realize that you are being crowned. Your auric field is being purified, and like the white butterflies, you are set free to explore the infinite circle of your Higher Self. The rainbow butterfly is offered to you as a bridge, connecting your life of service to the greater community, humanity, and the Earth evolving in the cosmos.

Child of Wands

Child of Wands
The Little Prince

It is often the little heartwarming gifts that make a profound difference in our lives. A gift may be freshly picked dandelions offered by a small child or a special gemstone brought by a friend from foreign shores. *The Little Prince*, written by Antoine de Saint-Exupéry, describes this truth in eloquent fashion through the character of the Little Prince. A small prince from a tiny planet visits the Earth and, with utter simplicity, transforms the life of a man who grows to understand the power of love. At the end of the story, as the Little Prince leaves him to go home to his own planet, he offers the man his star as a gift. The Little Prince says:

> All men have the stars, but they are not the same things for different people. For some, who are travelers, the stars are guides. For others they are no more than little lights in the sky. For others, who are scholars, they are problems. For my businessman they were wealth. But all these stars are silent. You—you alone—will have the stars as no one else has them. . . .
>
> In one of the stars I shall be living. In one of them I shall be laughing. And so it will be as if all the stars were laughing, when you look at the sky at night. . . . You—only you—will have stars that can laugh!

The Little Prince is the star child in each of us. As we open to the wonder of the stars, the flowers, and all of life in the universe, we humble ourselves to divine grace and spiritual protection. We, too, can travel to faraway places—

in our dreams and visions. We are able to visit exotic places right here on Earth and meet wonderful people in all corners of the globe.

The appearance of The Little Prince in your reading is a beautiful gift to you. The sweetest love is blossoming in your life. Climb aboard your butterfly of personal transformation and soar toward the awakened child of love that lives in your creative imagination. Take a moonlit walk and watch the twinkling stars. Do you see them smiling at you? Can you hear their childlike laughter?

Seeker of Wands

Seeker of Wands
Dorothy

> Somewhere over the rainbow, way up high, there's
> a land that I heard of, once in a lullaby. . . . A place you
> can get to without any trouble, it's far, far away, behind
> the Moon, beyond the rain.
>
> —*The Wizard of Oz* (movie)

Many of us have shared the magnificent dream of
Dorothy in *The Wizard of Oz*. A young girl from Kansas is
swept up in a tornado and has an inner journey as she ventures "off to see the wizard, the wonderful Wizard of Oz,"
a supposedly exalted being who may be able to direct her
back home. On her way, she encounters a good witch, a
wicked witch, three unique beings of varying character—
the Cowardly Lion, the Tin Man, and the Scarecrow—the
Munchkins, the Lollipop Kids, and others. Ultimately, she
finds her way home through the guidance of the Good Fairy
of the North. This angelic presence suggests to Dorothy that
the answer to her problem lies within. Dorothy later says, "If
I go looking for my heart's desire again, I won't look further
than my own backyard, because if it isn't there, I never really
lost it to begin with."

When Dorothy clicks her magic red shoes three times as
she repeats, "There's no place like home," it is symbolic of
wisdom—for the feet are the foundation and soul force of
the inner will and feelings. As we seek higher truth, often
our imagination and sense of adventure are stimulated, just
as the tornado shakes up the foundation of Dorothy's ex-

istence. When we set out on metaphysical journeys, we may find guides and helpers who love us and offer us wisdom along the way. We need dear and loyal friends on these adventures. Dorothy's nurturing relationship with her small dog, Toto, is symbolic of the dedication and family bonding that create a secure foundation on the path. Nevertheless, there are times when we travel toward a certain goal and realize that what we have been looking for has been within ourselves all the time. However, the journey itself is still essential.

When Dorothy appears in your reading, follow your destiny and proceed on your life quest. Develop your confidence and spiritual strength. You may be exploring and perceiving unusual realities at this time. Your dreams may be colorful, profound, fun, or adventurous. Keep a notebook of your nocturnal experiences. This may also be the time for an actual journey in the physical world. Open to the entire range of possible destinations. Take action to make your visions come true. Eliminate the fear of getting lost and making mistakes. Your helpers and guides will direct you home when your magical adventure is about to end.

Guide of Wands

Guide of Wands
The Pied Piper

When the town of Hamelin is infested with rats, a mysterious visitor known as the Pied Piper arrives. He says he will pipe the rats into the river for a fee, and the delighted town leaders agree. But after he completes the deed, the townspeople do not abide by their part of the contract. The Pied Piper is angry and decides to pipe an enchanting tune that mesmerizes all of Hamelin's children to follow him to a peaceful and serene mountain. However, one lame boy, attempting to keep up with the others, is shut out when the door to the mountain retreat closes before he can enter.

The message in this card is that you never know when the muse will suddenly arrive and depart. The muse is the spark of creative fire within the higher imagination. It can be subtle, fleeting, and tricky to understand. The lame boy represents the part of humanity touched by the muse and aware of its reality but still unable to find the way to manifest its power in the world. In the lame youth, we witness our need to discover the inner muse once we've been touched by its magic spell. He signifies our unique expression of divine wisdom, for he is unlike the other children. He is different, and we honor that distinctive quality when we honor the muse within.

The rats suggest the negative thoughts within the town's consciousness that require purification—cleansing in the river. The town won't pay the piper because the leaders are stuck in the realm of material values. They refuse to value the muse, the power of creative artistry. For their blindness and ignorance, they lose their future genius in the form of their children.

Eventually, the townspeople understand their failures. They name the main thoroughfare *Pied Piper Street* and build a stained-glass window in his honor. Later, a band of gypsies arrives in the town, and many of the older residents think it may be their lost children. The children have become inspired on their long journey. They have found their muse—symbolized by the Pied Piper—and have returned home to inspire their parents.

When the Pied Piper appears in your reading, it is time to follow your inner guide, your ingenious and inventive brand of thinking. Do not follow an outer leader piping a hypnotic tune; listen rather to the gentle refrains of your own inner music. Be playful. Dance. Sing. Let your artistic gifts blossom. Pay homage to the creative spirit that leads you forward on the path of life.

Guardian of Wands

Guardian of Wands
Raphael

In the mysterious and magical realm of spiritual life, there are said to be nine levels of immortal beings who encircle the Creator and offer guidance and protection to humanity and the many worlds of nature. The ancient names for these beings are seraphim, cherubim, thrones, dominions, virtues, powers, principalities, archangels, and angels. The four archangels are called Raphael, Michael, Gabriel, and Uriel.

Raphael, pictured on this card, is the archangel of providence who watches over humanity and offers direction and care to each struggling soul on Earth. When you need nurturance and protection, a guardian angel under the auspices of Raphael will comfort you. When you need divine wisdom to take the right fork in the road of life, an element of Raphael's towering presence can fill your heart and mind. The name *Raphael* actually means "God heals," and the first two letters, *Ra*, are reminiscent of the Egyptian name for the Sun God, Ra. This archangel is said to "rule" Sundays and can be understood more fully through various heart meditations. Through the centuries, this exalted being has been painted escorting a young man and his dog, reminding us of the guidance offered Dorothy and Toto in the Seeker of Wands.

The archangel Raphael is also a guardian to all travelers and people on religious and spiritual pilgrimages. Thus, he is often depicted with a staff and sandals. In *Inner Child*

Cards, his hands are shown blessing the Earth while a beautiful magic wand of soothing green forms his enormous wings. Raphael rules over the springtime and reveals his greatest gifts when the Sun is passing through fiery Aries (in March and April) while the Earth, which is in opposition to the Sun, moves through the harmonious vibrations of Libra.

When Raphael appears in your cards, you are being blessed by the presence of divine healing. Recognize the sensitive power in your hands that can rekindle strength in friends and family members. Send prayers and uplifting thoughts into the minds and hearts of human beings around the world. Visualize a stream of golden love emanating from the Sun, entering your heart chakra, and radiating out to your companions on the path of life. Travel with confidence. Make new friends. Cultivate your faith and express your compassion for all living things.

The Swords of Truth

The suit of swords is strongly connected with the air element in traditional tarot decks. The swords symbolize both the dynamic struggle of the ego's contradictions in the mental realm and the ability to cut through illusion and false ideologies. The ultimate significance of this suit is the honoring of truth not as a linear and rigid projection, but as a process or cycle. We do not find truth in parts, but in wholeness. The swords offer us the opportunity to examine the many facets of the human mind and its potential for clarity.

Since the mind can be active and bold, this suit is exemplified by knights, castles, dragons, and maidens. Throughout the evolution of the tarot, this suit has revealed images of struggle, disempowerment, grief, and conflict. The sword pictures in *Inner Child Cards* portray instead the qualities of valor and courage.

Swords are sharp and powerful. They can be used to protect, destroy, or conquer new territories. We use our minds in much the same way. Let these images speak to you about the way you use your mental abilities. Do they block or enhance your life? Adventure into this suit and discover the secret treasures concealed within the complex patterns of human thought.

Ace of Swords

Ace of Swords

Pictured in this card is the moment when King Arthur, as a teenage boy, pulled the magical sword Excalibur from an anvil at a tournament on New Year's Day. By this act, he became the rightful heir to the throne of Britain.

For ages, the sword has been a symbol of divine rulership and might. But it is much more than that. It represents the *spiritual will* that conquers fear and self-doubt. It is the strength of *clear thinking* that routs the mental armies of worry and indecision. It is the fiery force of *intuition*, an attribute of the higher mind that not every young person is capable of wielding. The magical nature of intuition allows a child to simply "know" a truth, a reality, or a situation directly, without recourse to rational thinking. When a youth pulls out and holds a magic sword, she or he is mentally empowered. Ultimately, with sword in hand, the young person follows her or his path of destiny, a warrior on the road of life. Down this winding road, each child learns an alphabet, words, sentences, and the fine art of speech—for human language is an extension of this sword of divine truth. Finally, as the child gains experience in the realm of swords, the sword itself can change—perhaps into a musical instrument, a staff of wisdom, a torch of enlightenment, or a fountain pen of inspirational wisdom.

When the Ace of Swords appears for you, tap into your power of one-pointed thinking. Seize hold of your divine will and wield it as a tool to vanquish negative thoughts. Remember that to live by fate is to be controlled by circumstances beyond your control. To "follow your destiny" is to honor your spiritual heritage and recognize that you came into this world for a clear purpose. By removing the sword from the stone, you are learning to explore your mental powers. The stone itself is the resistance of oppressive conditions. This card can indicate the birthing of a new way of thinking and the demise of illusions. It may signify the start of an intellectual project, the writing of a book, or the beginning of a journey.

Two of Swords

Two of Swords

Fencing and dueling are popular sports and art forms that require skill, balance, and grace. They involve lucid and quick movements coupled with the insight and awareness it takes to yield and surrender to one's opponent. Potentially, our minds can function in this fashion. However, in our stressful culture where dualistic thinking reigns, we inevitably get entangled in indecision and self-doubt. Resolving life's conflicts can become agonizing feats of battle. We often remain unyielding or unable to surrender to a difficult situation put before us.

This card offers the perspective that our mental conflicts can be experienced as a sport in which balance and wholeness are a priority. All of life is divided into opposites: yin/yang, male/female, light/dark, joy/sorrow. We must know one side in order to learn its polar complement. The crossed swords represent mental conflict. The radiant sun behind the swords is a reminder of the wholeness that overlights any form of dualism.

It may be a time in your life when you are making new decisions or searching for answers to old problems. Move toward your light and wisdom, and let the answers emerge like a great sunrise. Allow old worries to sink into the past like a poignant sunset. Clarity will come as you gently yield to the moment.

Three of Swords

Three of Swords

In this card, a beautiful young maiden is pictured playing a triangle crafted from tiny swords. She contemplates the prospect of harmony and focus. In an open window above, a songbird is perched on the sill, listening to her melody. This songbird symbolizes freedom.

Traditionally, the Three of Swords is a card of stress and confusion, often signaling lost love. However, what is actually lost is self-love, for the mind has lost contact with the heart. What is needed is a reunion of the heart chakra and the crown chakra in order that a symphony of thought can find a melodic message of truth within. The bird is a messenger liberating the girl from limiting thoughts. The number 3 signifies joy, harmony, and communication. The triangle also symbolizes the spiritual trinity of spirit, heart, and body. The girl is learning how to "play with" and blend these three aspects of human existence. The castle walls suggest the mental constructs that block true expression of beautiful soul qualities in the world.

Remember that your thoughts are your allies. Learn to play your thoughts like an orchestra. Your fears might be the drums, your hopes the violins, and your victories the trumpets. Seek the pure joy of the mind. Don't let the refrains of self-doubt cause mental discord. Your daily language can be as magnificent as a finely tuned Mozart concerto. On a practical level, this card may suggest bringing more music into your life. Play a musical instrument or listen to a favorite recording. The magic of sound can be a healing force—soothing your mind, calming your emotions, and relaxing your body.

Four of Swords

Four of Swords

While we are young, we are especially open to the currents of sudden change and new direction in life. At crucial stages of development, an individual begins to construct thoughts in a more meaningful way. In this card, inner truth—represented by the stream—accompanied by the desire to understand freedom—the raft—emerges from the watery depths of the past—the fishing swords or lines. The raft is a metaphor for a mind newly constructed upon the idea that budding consciousness is yet to be found. The hope for higher knowledge is seen in the distance, only partially visible. In this card, freedom and form are a graceful pair, represented by the white bird that leads the boys on their journey.

Fishing is often a relaxing activity, as is floating down a stream on a raft. As you seek to retrieve memory images from the unconscious realm in order to build your future, strive to duplicate the quiet rhythm of the river you see in this card. Do not rush your process. Imagine yourself to be a fisherman, deepening your knowledge and dropping your line into the unknown waters of life. Anticipate the big catch. This stage of mental maturation can begin at any age. It comes when we feel the urge to build a new foundation of awareness.

A time for rest or more tranquil surroundings may enhance the quality of your life. Be at peace as you enter the waters of deep change and initiation.

Five of Swords

Five of Swords

In the Five of Swords, the river raft of the Four of Swords finds a place to dock, and the fishing rod or sword is firmly secured in the sand. The boy leaves the raft behind and begins to explore a variety of uncovered truths that are awaiting him. He gazes at a starfish, which reveals the potential of his creative mind. In numerology, the number 5 is connected with freedom, adventure, and unexpected changes on the path of life. The seals on the shore symbolize the emergence of unseen life forces coming to the boy. His awareness is fresh as he discovers new ideas. Most exciting is the realization that clarity is brilliantly emerging like the bright sun in the sky behind him.

As you venture from your raft of the past, be aware of the truth and freedom that await you. Freedom misused can be confusing and chaotic. Be thoughtful and discriminating as you gather resources and information. Know your boundaries—the lessons of the raft. Clarify your goals. The boy is on a slippery rock, and he must move carefully to stay surefooted. Anticipate illuminating insights from places deep within you. This is a creative and purposeful time. Most importantly, focus your attention and thoughts.

Six of Swords

Six of Swords

The grand and dramatic salute pictured in this card is a tribute to the active force of the mind that has found unity and success. Each child holds a cup, representing the heart force, and a sword, representing the mind force. The destination has been reached, and the search for new clarity is complete. There is focus and a unified vision. There is responsibility, loyalty, and friendship. At this level of exalted awareness, the individual has merged with the ideal of community. From this union, the mission to serve the planet is possible. The heightened mind, symbolized by the swords, is infused with light. The mind is brilliant and full of triumph.

You have reached a pinnacle. Foresight and inspiration have embraced your mind, and it is as if warm sunlight is evaporating the waters of negative thinking and fear. Salute! Sit up straight, close your eyes, and let the light of the solar fire become an elixir of wisdom. A golden aura of divine protection surrounds you. Now is the time to serve humanity with clear vision.

Seven of Swords

Seven of Swords

In this card, a young scholar has begun the task of unraveling sacred knowledge. This marks a period of contemplation. The child gazes out the window to view a peaceful setting in which a ship sails by in the distance. This is symbolic, for it reflects the expanded horizon that lies before him. His pens are in the shape of tiny swords that aid him in inscribing the truth and clarity that are emerging from his solitude. The books before him are a source of ancient teachings. As a symbol of mysticism, the scroll represents time. The part of the scroll that is unrolled is the present, and the unrolled paper at either end is the enshrouded past and the unknown future. The symbols in this card represent study, enlightenment, and communication.

It may be time to begin new studies or rekindle your love for a special project or field of research. This is a quiet and reflective time. Inner guidance is at work. Activities like reading books, writing papers, and exploring your imagination are enhanced. Appreciate and honor your time alone. You may want to learn more about meditation, contemplation, and visualization techniques. Most of all, find a place of peace within yourself.

Eight of Swords

Eight of Swords

The children in the Eight of Swords card are walking through a cave or labyrinth that represents a soul journey into unknown territories. A labyrinth often has one winding path that leads toward an ultimate goal. It is often used in initiatic procedures. When deep transformation occurs, we are often guided into the secret places of our minds in order to resolve old karmic patterns and subliminal fears. Oriental mystics say that the true self resides in the cave of the heart. We must go there to restore our wisdom.

The spider represents the enigma of the web, which weaves in and out of itself. Our minds are similar. We reshape and recreate our thoughts continuously. The snake, coiled in a figure eight—the symbol of infinity—is the psychic power and life force within. This snake reminds us of the ancient kundalini energy wisdom that travels up and down our spines, and has been likened to a fiery dragon sleeping within the root chakra. The ability to readapt in life situations is essential if we are to successfully respond to the calling for change and maturation.

You may feel that this is a trying time in your life. Put worries aside, for you are entering a sacred journey. Overcoming fear is possible if you are willing to confront its deceptive face. Perhaps you are not honoring this time of initiation. The way to do so is to illuminate the deep fears that block your life and be ready to come to terms with their potent meanings. This is a unique opportunity to clean the house of your psyche. There is always light at the end of a tunnel.

Nine of Swords

Nine of Swords

Seated in a grassy meadow, the child on this card finds himself enclosed by nine swords. Symbolically, he is unable to see beyond the limiting mental constructs (the swords) that he has created for himself. He is also encircled by a whimsical dragon, his unrecognized ally whom he has unknowingly made into an enemy. When this youth is ready to look up and face the dragon, he will realize that this beast is a powerful and yet unintegrated aspect of himself.

The number 9 denotes completion. Old thoughts are ready to dissipate. In time, one by one, the swords will come down as the child opens to the loving process of letting the dragon in. However, the swords must be honored, for they are protecting the boy from the pain and wisdom that he is unprepared to assimilate. In Chinese Taoist symbolism, the dragon is revered as a spirit showing "the way."

Seek the imaginative dragon in yourself, and let it guide you toward a transformed vision of your future goals. Be aware of how you armor yourself with limiting thoughts or rigid ideas. Be willing to complete the cycle of entrapment by opening gently and lovingly to an expanded view of your life.

Ten of Swords

Ten of Swords

Triumph and liberation are in the air. The fully knighted youth in this card has come to accept his inner power. In the Nine of Swords, the dragon holds the boy captive because the boy is unable to see beyond his fear. In the Ten of Swords, the dragon is encircled by the boy's swords, symbolizing his integration of the power and courage he needs to overcome terror and oppression. As he inserts the tenth sword into the ground, a circle is formed around the dragon signifying that he has attained a unity of mind, spirit, and matter.

You are now free to explore the start of a new cycle of conscious awareness. You have worked very hard to overcome mental blocks and tensions. You understand more about the courage it requires to cleanse the mind of negative thoughts, for you have faced your dragon. The circle of life continues, and you are now ready for a new round of adventures. When a future crisis arises, you will know what to do. Use the wisdom and experience you have gained from the past and remember to nurture yourself along the path. The mind is very powerful. You must infuse it with kind and loving thoughts. You deserve a star of accomplishment.

Child of Swords

Child of Swords
Pinocchio

May Lamberton Becker, in her introduction to *Pinocchio*, quotes the philosopher Benedetto Croce, who said that the "wood out of which Pinocchio is carved is humanity itself." This reminds us that all human beings make mistakes as we struggle to fulfill our greatest dreams. Children love Pinocchio because he is so much like them.

A poor carpenter named Gepetto, while carving a puppet, discovers one morning that the wooden doll he has crafted can speak and has become a rude and selfish young boy with a long nose that grows as he tells lies. As the story unfolds, Pinocchio has many lessons to learn about truth and integrity. He wants to go to school and study, but he is tempted to "follow the music"—that is, follow his muse—and stray from the path of education. Eventually, through his many misadventures in the world, he learns about the virtues of selfless love and service to humanity.

Pinocchio's lessons are the same ones we learn while we grow into maturity. Young children are tempted to lie and steal to extricate themselves from everyday problems. Pinocchio's mind is still developing, and he has not yet understood the importance of truth and honor. He has not yet had to face himself in the mirror of life.

When we begin to outgrow some form of youthful ignorance, the Pinocchio card may come up. At this point, we are no longer marionettes dancing to the strings of desire and greed but humans reaching toward a mature outlook on life. Pinocchio achieves his dream of becoming truly humane when he sacrifices his own desires for the love and healing of his maker, Gepetto.

If the Child of Swords appears in your reading, you are being asked to investigate the power of truth in your life. How honest are you? Make a clean break with any long-standing patterns of lying, cheating, and self-deception. See yourself clearly in the mirror that reveals your true features. Learn to use the spiritual willpower and mental discipline of the sword to stay on your path of destiny.

Seeker of Swords

Seeker of Swords
The Scarecrow

Both Pinocchio and The Wizard of Oz's Scarecrow are not fully human, but they are created by humans. They are striving to develop the power to think for themselves. As the Scarecrow introduces himself, he is completely lacking in direction and says, "I can't even scare a crow." Later on, as he moves along the Yellow Brick Road, the Scarecrow becomes quite resourceful and clever. It appears that the journey or quest itself educates the Scarecrow, drawing out his knowledge. When he meets with the wizard, the Scarecrow realizes that his own wits and intelligence are fully present. When Dorothy is ready to go home, she turns to her beloved man of straw and says, "Scarecrow, I'll miss you the most." This suggests the dignity and importance of the intellect and clear thinking.

In the Seeker of Swords card, the two swords represent the lack of purpose, mental conflict, and dualistic thought that will eventually be harmonized. The sunflowers signify the potential to fulfill one's destiny, to rise up in all humility and bow down before the radiance of the lifegiving Sun. The Scarecrow himself is portrayed as a giant sunflower trying to cultivate the willpower and clarity of thought he will eventually find while learning life's lessons on the Yellow Brick Road.

The Scarecrow has an innocence and naiveté about him. His carefree and spontaneous nature reminds us of The Fool or court jester until he realizes his task: to outwit the Wicked Witch and help Dorothy on her mission. At that point, he is ready to utilize his mind in service to the greater whole. He grows away from selfishness and toward dedication to his companions. The Scarecrow's brain changes from a seed of personal enlightenment into a flower of divine compassion.

When the Scarecrow appears in your cards, feel more confident about your mental abilities. If necessary, build your vocabulary, read the dictionary, learn a new language, or study the literary classics. Take a positive step to enrich your intellectual universe. Avoid hesitation and indecision. Golden opportunities are always available for the person with foresight and wisdom.

Guide of Swords

Guide of Swords
Robin Hood

Robin Hood and his merry men lived in twelfth-century England. They were outlaw heroes to the native Saxons of Sherwood Forest, stealing from the rich Norman lords and giving the proceeds to the poor peasants who worked the land. The true Robin Hood was actually a brilliant archer and swordsman who became a legend in his own time. His exploits with Little John, Will Scarlet, Friar Tuck, Allan A-Dale, and even King Richard the Lion-Hearted, have become tales of adventure that continue to stir the minds and hearts of young people from all corners of the world. The experiences of these merry men link us to the magical days of King Arthur and the Knights of the Round Table, and to the experiences of Jesus and his twelve disciples.

During a time of governmental corruption and political intrigue, Robin Hood and his band became symbols of justice, humanitarian service, and goodwill. The Guide of Swords represents a true merging of understanding, cleverness, and love for one's people or community. That which was solely potential in the Pinocchio card and a partial realization in the Scarecrow card has become a way of life in the Robin Hood card.

Robin Hood's love for Maid Marian presents another dimension within the realm of the Swords: spiritual union and physical marriage blessed by a dedication to upholding the laws of nature. In France, nearly three centuries after

Robin Hood, another Guide of Swords came forth to lead a nation out of slavery and toward the light offered by the Archangel Michael. That Guide of Swords was Joan of Arc.

In this card, Robin Hood reveals the Sword of Truth by his side and the arrows of higher consciousness and goal-orientation in a quiver on his back. He has just retrieved the gold that several rich aristocrats had essentially stolen from the poor by overtaxing and burdening them.

When Robin Hood is present in your reading, be determined to follow in his footsteps. Seize the initiative on your life path. Help the needy. Be generous to the poor. Teach others about the values of justice, fairness, equality, and honor. Explore the forests and learn to live in harmony with nature. Remember the ancient adage "The truth will set you free."

Guardian of Swords

Guardian of Swords
Michael

The Archangel Michael has always been considered to be the captain of Christ's armies, the commander of the heavenly hosts. He was almost certainly the "angel with the drawn sword" who appeared to Joshua before the Battle of Jericho, when the trumpets were sounded, the walls came tumbling down, and the Sun stood still. In Revelation, he was said to lead thousands of angels with his flaming sword in the apocalyptic battle against the ancient dragon, representing Satan, the fallen angels, and the demons. Michael is the celestial personification of spiritual might and willpower. If you need to protect your mind from negative thoughts and confusion, a prayer to an angel under Michael's auspices will comfort you. When it's time to summon extra courage to face an important decision in your life, the overlighting guidance of Michael will illuminate a path of truth for you to follow.

The name *Michael* actually means "who is like God." He is the archangel who has charge over the Roman Catholic Church. While Michael has provided divine inspiration to thousands of soldiers, knights, and warriors through the ages, he is not responsible for the evil deeds and excesses that are committed by men of free will in times of war and conflict. Michael attempts to instill in humanity the sense of God's awesome, creative power to manifest goodwill on Earth. His greatest strength is felt when the Sun travels through Libra (in September and October) while the Earth, in opposition to the Sun, is passing through fiery Aries.

In this card, an armored Michael reveals his towering presence over our planet. The Sword of Truth, mental clarity, and goodwill is offered in friendship. This card also reminds us of the Way of the Cross—the pain and suffering we must bear throughout many lifetimes as we serve our friends and companions. The red rose suggests the eventual flowering of humanity and the mystic fellowship of planetary warriors who have sworn eternal allegiance to the Christ of universal love.

When Michael makes his presence known to you, you may be weary from one of life's many battles. Rekindle your passion to live according to the highest truth possible. The spirit of honesty and righteousness is upon you. Remember Jesus' words in the Garden of Gethsemane shortly before his crucifixion: "Not my will, but thy will be done." During a contemplative interlude, your own faith and belief in higher powers can be restored. Walk the path of life with humility, confidence, a heart of gold, and noble intentions.

The Winged Hearts

The Winged Hearts of *Inner Child Cards* correspond to the water suit in the traditional tarot, which is called the cups. They symbolize the feminine, receptive quality of the heart that encompasses our feelings, emotions, dreams, and our love-nature. They are in rhythm with the mysterious cycles of the Moon.

The Winged Heart is a divine symbol representing the freedom offered by unconditional love. The Sufis, who tap the essence of Islam as well as of all religions, use this symbol as an emblem of love and devotion.

The mermaids, mermen, and underwater scenes illustrated throughout this suit characterize the unconscious forces that lie beneath the surface of our everyday awareness. They also represent the hidden magic of the dream world that forms a major part of our creative imaginations. Mermaids are said to live in springs, rivers, and in oceans, guarding the treasures of undersea palaces. They serve as guardians and protectors of love. They come to heal and nurture. They beckon us to search the myriad of riches that are buried within the cave of the heart. The key to this suit is opening to the higher potentials of human and divine love.

Ace of Hearts

Ace of Hearts

The essence of true love is, above all, faith—in the ineffable reverence that grows out of the union with a beloved. This beloved can be your inner self or another human soul. The root meaning of love is to acknowledge absolute concern for another being. In order to express this empathy for another, one must secure self-love in one's own heart.

In this card, two mermaids joyously push a Winged Heart up from the sea. It is offered as an inspired sunrise, touching the golden light of the sky. This heart reveals the acceptance of love at the highest level, for the heart is the vessel of life, adorned with wings of spiritual freedom.

An ace in any suit is always positive. This card affirms that a new opportunity in the realm of love is rising out of the depths of the past, symbolized by the ocean. This new love may be a person, an idea, the realization of a dream, or a new creative endeavor. Open your heart to what this card offers you, because it holds the key to exploring the higher dimensions of universal love. Have faith in love, for it can comfort you in times of crisis. Love is like an eternal flame whose steady light can always guide you during times of personal darkness. Love is always there, and will never abandon you.

Two of Hearts

Two of Hearts

Sacred union and attraction in the feeling realm are personified by the mermaid and merman in this card. A rainbow connects and balances them. Two dolphins representing the intelligence of the universe leap over the rainbow in unison and joy. According to classical myth, the dolphin was placed among the stars as the constellation Delphinius because it played the role of matchmaker, merging the sea goddess Amphitrite with Poseidon. This card can symbolize either two people sharing love or two aspects of a person striving for unity and wholeness. Therefore, marriage, in all its forms, is associated with this card.

It is from this place of divine union that we encounter balance and integrity in the polarity of the sexes. Two in any suit attracts the potential to regulate duality. You may be sharing your heart with another at this time, one whom you feel to be a beloved mate. This spiritual partner could be an actual lover, a friend, or a higher awakening. As you meditate on the deeper meanings of this card, remember that your own heart can be a rainbow bridge of living color and light, linking you to the source of the Divine Child within and helping you heal old wounds in the heart of a loved one.

Three of Hearts

Three of Hearts

Ancient Goddess worshipers claimed that the creation of the universe stemmed from the mysterious rhythm and magic dance of the deep waters. Oriental mystics said that the true self, identical to the eternally dancing deity, resides in the cave of the heart. This connection between the heart and the Higher Self is an important facet in the evolving flow and harmony of life.

In this card, a happy clam sends up bubbles of laughter as a buried treasure chest containing vast riches and jewels rests unopened. Two joyous sea beings frolic to the magical sounds emanating from a shell harp played by a third sea being, a mermaid. Tantric tradition calls rhythm the sound of power or the heartbeat of the absolute. This beating sound is perceptible when one plunges into the depths of consciousness. The Three of Hearts is a jubilant call, arousing in you the spirit of play, imagination, and eternal friendship.

As you discover the little child who resides in your heart, let your feelings bubble up. Let this child know how much it is loved and cherished. Honor the intimate dance that you and this child share. Some tears of joy may flow. This card may also signify a celebration or party. The number 3 symbolizes the coming together of friends and family. Listen to the music, and don't forget to dance.

Four of Hearts

Four of Hearts

Sunken treasures, lost hopes, broken hearts, and tearful goodbyes are all aspects of the emotional journey one must encounter in life. Though these times are painful, the ever-transforming tides of hope exist within them. A broken heart is an open heart. When we are willing to allow deep emotions to flow, there is invariably a gift of love at the other side. Sorrow brings the tidings of joy. This is the bittersweet aspect of love.

The gentle mermaid in this card has lost her hope. The boat she was guiding during a storm has sunk, and her Winged Heart locket is broken. In time, she will look up and see her three friends, riding on dolphins, coming to her rescue. What seems lost will be regained a thousand times over as she reconstructs and discovers a new foundation of faith and hope in herself and in life.

Often, we cannot see the forest for the trees. Treasures that lie before us cannot be found until we are able to discover them. This card may be describing an emotional situation for you. Allow yourself the time to feel these emotions. Honor your process of introspection. With faith and hope, a new revelation will gently come forward to heal your broken heart. Becoming one with your feelings is a crucial step on the path of life.

Five of Hearts

Five of Hearts

Often, during our darkest hours, there is a need for reflection and rest, represented in this card by the sea turtles, the calm ocean, and the crescent Moon. Then, suddenly, something magical can happen. The mermaid of the Four of Hearts who experiences sorrow and hopeless feelings opens a treasure chest in the Five of Hearts, and is offered a special Winged Heart. She gazes at a golden pentacle at the center of this heart, a symbolic star of initiation reflecting her cosmic guiding star in the heavens. The pentacle is the most widely revered of all esoteric symbols. Traditionally, its meaning refers to the perfection of humanity. The pentacle can act as a spiritual protector and is connected to the mystical significance of the number 5. The main quality inherent in this number is that of change. In this card, the mermaid is experiencing a change of heart: she is healing the wounds of the past.

When change occurs in your life, especially at an emotional level, you may feel confused and vulnerable. The changes now happening in your life are guided and protected by the seal of the golden star residing at the center of your heart. This star is your Higher Self. Rest assured that creativity will follow this interlude of chaos. Don't let the blues get you down. Anticipate a renewal of both interpersonal and divine love.

Six of Hearts

Six of Hearts

It is an ancient belief that storks are heralds of new life. They are seen frequenting ponds and marshes, which has given rise to the belief that the spirits of unborn children wait in these places, seeking a new mother or a new life. Thus, storks are known as soul carriers.

In this card, something holy is occurring. Five mermaids are joining with each other and rising from the sea. The sixth mermaid, flying upon a stork, is offering a spiritual lifeline from above. In ecstasy, the five emerge from the ocean, representing the unconscious, into the air and sunlight, representing higher revelations. They rejoice as they touch one another and reach skyward. A transition is taking place. It is as if emotions have surfaced and are now being released.

Imagine that the sea has claimed your tears and the Sun is drying your eyes. This is an inner healing, and one that you deserve. The number 6 represents support, dedication, responsibility, and unity. It can also signify the need to balance your emotional life. This may be the time for a family healing or resolution of a conflict with a loved one. A deep, heartfelt connection with your friends or community may be happening.

Seven of Hearts

Seven of Hearts

Seven is a mystical number representing visions, dreams, and contemplation. It is associated with the seven chakras, the seven colors of the rainbow, the seven pillars of wisdom in the Middle East, the "Seven Sisters" of the Pleiades, and the seven stars of the Big Dipper in the constellation of The Great Bear (Ursa Major). The peaceful mermaid in this card meditates below an arch of seven Winged Hearts in a submerged Atlantean temple. She wears a seven-pointed star symbolizing the light of spiritual protection and guidance. In a sense, she is stargazing.

When you meditate on universal truths and secrets, you can expand your consciousness beyond the boundaries of time and space. Often, at this point, you become aware of the divine abundance that lives within your heart as well as a greater need for focus and clarity. This may be a time to withdraw your physical energies and settle into the "spiritual here and now."

Reacquaint yourself with the power of hidden resources and balance your outer desires with your inner needs. Take time to be alone and nurture your soul. Create your own little world or sanctuary where external chaos cannot intrude. Sweet messages can come to you in these heartfelt moments.

Eight of Hearts

Eight of Hearts

The infinity symbol stands for completeness. It is composed of a solar right side and a lunar left side and can denote union or balance between the sexes. In essence, it is two becoming one. Ancient mystics said this symbol indicated the presence of twin gods or goddesses. Such twins were praised as magicians, healers, and angels of fertility.

In this card, twin water spirits are uniting through the deep, transforming circle of power and change. Although their music is calm, the waves behind them ebb and flow with a rhythm of strength and force. This is represented by the eight musical notes in the shape of Winged Hearts.

The blending of these opposing forces is the key to understanding personal transformation. The number 8 is itself a sign for infinity and represents passion, sexuality, power, and regeneration. Realize that you have both male and female energies within your psyche. If each of us were to consciously use our gifts of sexuality and empowerment constructively, together we would create a safer and less destructive world. This card asks you to find spiritual and emotional equilibrium within the realm of feelings. A profound change awaits you when you integrate a personal sense of empowerment with a serene understanding of the universal flow of life. Inner harmony can lead you to a state of divine bliss and actualize your potential as a gifted healer.

Nine of Hearts

Nine of Hearts

A well, vessel, or cauldron can hold sacred waters for rituals, blessings, purifications, and healings. Water is the essence of all life. The answer to the question of whether the cup is half full or half empty depends on how life is being viewed at a given moment. This question is being asked of you now.

Along with this question, you may be granted a wish. In the traditional tarot, the Nine of Hearts is often considered the "wish card." Your wish should reflect what you feel you deserve in life, where your heart is, and how much you love yourself. Wishing is a way to observe how well you are seeking your individual fulfillment. Can you accept a happy life? This is not an easy question to answer, and much care should go into this inquiry. Sometimes wounds of the past must be healed before you can grow into your wish. Forgiveness of self and others is one step toward greater fulfillment.

The mermaid in this card is holding her vessel toward the waterfall to be filled. She has reached a point of acceptance in her life and is ready to have her cup run over. Hold your own cup high toward the waters of life and dare to fill it completely. Imagine the possibility of unlimited love, joy, and wisdom pouring into your heart. This may be a time for spiritual initiation or purification in your life. Believe in miracles, and follow your dreams.

Ten of Hearts

Ten of Hearts

There is a time when you reach a symbolic pot of gold or feel the multicolored rainbow of hope in your heart. This is a moment or transition when a heartfelt "Thank you!" can be offered to the overlighting angels who guide and protect you through the years.

In this card, nine Winged Hearts illuminate the aura of a jubilant mermaid as a tenth heart appears upon her forehead, signifying the opening of her third eye or *ajna* center. She is awakened to feelings of love and devotion for humanity. The number *10* in this suit represents the powerful transformation that inevitably leads to emotional rebirth.

Your wishes and dreams may have come true, or you may be striving to reach an important goal at this time. A special responsibility must be accepted as you seek to fill your cup, for it is at this point that personal fulfillment can be poured back into the greater whole of humanity. This will allow you to be open to the spiritual waters of universal love and divine healing. You may then offer these beautiful gifts to your family, the greater community, and the planet. Hold your arms up to the sky and let waves of exalted joy fill your heart.

Child of Hearts

Child of Hearts
Goldilocks

In our eternal quest for shelter and safety, we are often curious about the heart-centered lives or soul qualities of other beings. In the story "Goldilocks and the Three Bears," we are introduced to an orderly existence of bear sizes, porridge bowls, chairs, and beds. The bears have designed a ritualistic system that creates a rather fixed, yet natural and harmonious way of life.

Goldilocks represents a child's curiosity, innocence, and eagerness while searching for a true sense of home, identity, and family ties. She peers into the bears' cottage through a window symbolizing the universal eye or looking glass that mirrors back greater wisdom. Goldilocks is the child in each of us, the Child of Hearts who gains a beautiful vision of another world.

For a few moments, she is so intrigued by this realm that she feels safe enough to try the bears' food, sit in their chairs, and even sleep in their beds; her sensitive heart finds a temporary resting place. However, as the bears return from their daily travels, they discover the intruder in their home. Goldilocks runs away when she is discovered. She creates a crisis in the existing order, but learns a major lesson about nurturance, safety, and kinship.

When Goldilocks appears in your reading, open your childlike heart to the spirit of home and hearth. Be more accepting about a loved one's lifestyle. Explore your in-depth feelings with a sense of exuberance and wonder. See the world from a new vantage point. Realize that the three bears' sense of organization and structure may reflect your own behavior patterns and crystalized habits. A guest or friend may be coming to visit you. Will you scare away this new companion or welcome the person with open arms?

Seeker of Hearts

Seeker of Hearts
The Tin Man

When Dorothy meets the Tin Man in *The Wizard of Oz*, he is very stiff. The tinsmith, his creator, has forgotten to give him a heart. He desperately needs to be oiled, signifying the blocked emotions causing his rigidity and pain. During the course of the story, the Tin Man cries. His tears, which had made him rust before, are like the flow of oil—the elixir of love and sorrow that heals the wounds of the past. On the Yellow Brick Road, the Tin Man seeks a heart with which to love, be joyful, dance, and sing. However, the Wizard tells him he doesn't know how lucky he is *not* to have a heart. "Hearts will never be practical until they can be made unbreakable," he suggests. But the Tin Man still wants his heart because without it he will never be fully human. The wizard offers him one more pearl of wisdom: "A heart is not judged by how much you love, but how much you are loved by others."

In the Seeker of Hearts, the Tin Man wears a suit of armor, shielding and protecting him from the strange world of feelings. His horse suggests the freedom of the soul, carrying the Tin Man on his important life quest. The dove, a divine messenger of peace and tranquillity, carries the heart that will make the Tin Man a true member of evolving humanity.

When the Tin Man appears in your reading, be more open hearted. Rejoice in your opportunity to experience an initiation into the realm of feelings, devotion, and compassion. Remember to express your emotions. To cry is to reveal the pain that lives within the core of every human soul. Be a seeker of hearts and find ways to uplift friends and relatives in trouble. As a warrior of universal love, you have a special gift of the spirit to offer every person you meet on the path of life.

Guide of Hearts

Guide of Hearts
The Good Fairy

During times of distress or those extreme turning points of life known as "the dark nights of the soul," we may lose sight of our guides and teachers. Seemingly bereft of any tangible support, we may feel completely lost, at our wits' end. Then, perhaps at the eleventh hour, a ray of light and hope comes shining through. The answer to our prayers arrives in a lightninglike flash, or a visitation from a nurturing spirit offers us liberation.

In *The Wizard of Oz*, the Good Fairy of the North plays a small role but one that is vital and of central importance. As a guardian angel to Dorothy, the Good Fairy patiently waits behind the scenes, watching the young girl's adventures and looking out for her welfare. She allows Dorothy to learn her own lessons, which she tells her near the end of the story.

Dorothy is still perplexed about how to return to her Auntie Em and the farmhouse when the Scarecrow, signifying the mind and reason, looks up and sees the Good Fairy coming. The Good Fairy tells Dorothy that she has always had the power to go back to Kansas. All she has to do is click her magic shoes three times and repeat, "There's no place like home." Life's greatest riddles are always locked away in our hearts. If we follow the path of the heart, we will know what to do and when to do it.

In the Guide of Hearts card, the wizard, hoping to take Dorothy home, has accidentally left the Earth in his balloon, leaving the young girl behind. Simultaneously, the

Good Fairy of the North arrives from the heavens, waving her celestial wand and restoring Dorothy's faith in her own magical powers.

When the Good Fairy appears in your reading, love is being sent to you by invisible helpers and angelic spirits. Don't despair if a problem seems unresolvable. Believe in yourself. Quiet your mind, and let an intuitive answer materialize within your imagination. A symbol, an archetype, or a special person may be your link to happiness. Remember the old saying "Home is where the heart is." Realize that you can be a disguised Good Fairy at heart. Your soothing words, gentle touch, or inspirational example can lead a friend or loved one out of darkness and into light.

Guardian of Hearts

Guardian of Hearts
Gabrielle

Archangel Gabriel—who in this card receives a feminine expression as Gabrielle—is the chief revealer of divine mysteries to humanity. It was this archangel who helped Daniel interpret dreams and visions in the lion's den. Gabriel also came to Zecharias, announcing that John the Baptist would soon be born. And this mighty celestial ambassador came to Mary, saying that her child, Jesus, would be the Messiah who had been long awaited by the Jewish people. In Revelation, it is Gabriel who blows the trumpet of rebirth, asking human beings to rise out of their antipathy and embrace each other in selfless love and compassion.

The name *Gabriel* actually means "hero of God." Often depicted carrying a lily, scepter, or holy scroll, this archangel brings glad tidings to the faithful as well as judgment or mercy to those who have committed sins and evil deeds. Gabriel helps human beings unite their spirits and bodies through heart-centered revelations and insights. Gabriel impregnates the human soul with a vision of divine wisdom, hoping to stir the personality into a life of greater devotion and service. This archangel's greatest strength occurs while the Sun transits through Capricorn, and the Earth, in opposition to the Sun, is passing through watery Cancer. Gabriel is strongly connected to the magical lunar realm, the cycles of life, and oceanic currents.

In this card, a rainbow-winged Gabrielle is the Guardian of Hearts. She is a golden-haired mermaid sounding the harmonious music that will bring seals and other sea creatures to the surface world. She carries the Holy Grail of universal love and human kindness.

When Gabrielle appears in your reading, hear the call to spiritual rebirth. Watch your dreams for inspiring symbols and stories that ask you to awaken to a higher life. Be compassionate to those individuals who seem most vulnerable and down on their luck. You can be a teacher whose words, songs, and gentle touch heal loved ones. Build a rainbow bridge of trust and understanding to your friends around the world.

The Earth Crystals

The Earth Crystals correspond to the traditional earth suit in the tarot known as disks or pentacles. They represent the physical plane, or material bodies, money, and security. The crystals offer many perspectives about how we are manifesting our abundance.

Crystals were often referred to in ancient times as the veins of the earth, frozen water, or frozen light. Our physical bodies and the Earth we live on can be greatly healed by the use of crystals.

In German folklore, gnomes are considered the nature spirits associated with the earth element. They are said to live in mines, caves, and mountains, and beneath trees and forests. They have miraculous knowledge and power regarding crystals, gems, and minerals. They serve as guardian spirits who strengthen the foundations of the planet.

The gnomes pictured throughout this suit offer another view of human life. The cards portray gnome children, parents, and elders working, playing, and creating a beautiful world out of earthly delights. In many ways, these gnomes symbolize the family of humanity and the world of nature joining together in harmony.

Ace of Crystals

Ace of Crystals

In northern folklore and legend, a belief exists that during the winter months when the Earth is silent and asleep, under her blanket of snow the gnomes are busy weaving crystals from the light of the Moon, Sun, and stars. When the rebirth of springtime arrives, the gnomes offer these precious gems to the sky, and through the gentle rain of springtime, magnificent rainbows are created.

The hardworking gnome in this card has uncovered a beautiful crystal for you. The time has come for you to accept the promise of hope, unity, and abundance that this crystal brings. The rainbow in the sky is a bridge uniting heaven and Earth and representing the harmony of all people. The Chinese called the rainbow the *t'ai chi*, or "Great Ultimate," uniting yin and yang.

When the Ace of Crystals appears in your reading, great potential is being uncovered and tremendous possibilities are present in your life, for this card depicts a dynamic rebirth on the physical level. You may be birthing something magical, be it a baby, a business, a book, a relationship, or a new phase of self-expression. You are blessed by the presence of the glorious crystal brought to you by this humble gnome. An ace in any suit says, "Yes!" Begin anew. Many ideas and dreams that have been hidden for years are now revealed. Join the light of a new day. Blessed be.

Two of Crystals

Two of Crystals

Balance is an integral part of the philosophy of ancient cultures. It is so important that it is represented in the zodiacal sign Libra. This sign represents justice, fairness, poise, equilibrium, and cooperation.

The gnome children in this card are playing a favorite game of seesaw. In order to enjoy this game, the little gnomes must observe the rules of balance and cooperation; otherwise, the game can become dangerous. The empty swing in the background represents the independent activity of one person. On the seesaw, two people have come together—symbolizing the union of male and female qualities—to learn the lessons of polarity and relationship. If they are to succeed, they must work as a team and support one another.

This card represents the first stage of conscious interaction. The owl, which is perched at the center of the log, signifies the wisdom of the middle ground that must be reached when individuals search for understanding and equality in relationship. Inherent in this card is the need for interpersonal sharing and the acknowledgment that ups and downs are a vital part of everyday life. This process is internal as well as external. The key is a flowing pattern that is beneficial to all concerned.

Take good care of yourself, your relationships, and your health when you receive this card. Exercising mind, body, and spirit can bring you the agility to incorporate balance, whether you are alone or with a partner. Life can seem like a seesaw existence, but you can still have a wonderful time if you maintain a playful attitude.

Three of Crystals

Three of Crystals

Jump rope takes three or more people to play and is one of several childhood games that stimulates rhyme, song, and laughter. The game synthesizes active and passive behavior as children take turns holding the rope and jumping in the center. In many ways, this reflects the laws of community at their best. All participants are needed to create a rhythm of steady movement. The number 3 represents group activity, communication, and joy.

This card symbolizes community spirit and the fulfillment achieved when all parties are personally involved. The jump rope pictured here is a rainbow representing the bridge or arc that can lead to world harmony.

When the Three of Crystals appears in your reading, it may be time for you to redefine your purpose in the community and joyfully share the wisdom and gifts that you have to offer. Join groups. Get to know families and children in your neighborhood. Share your life with like-minded individuals who cherish and respect your view of life. If you have not found your group or a special circle of friends, now would be a fruitful time to deepen your inner joy in order to strengthen your self-confidence and personal resources. Above all else, remember to play.

Four of Crystals

Four of Crystals

It is important to discover the center of gravity within the soul, that magical core that draws forth creative will. This empowerment helps us build the world according to our deepest values and guiding principles. Personal responsibility and constructive actions are beginning steps toward the foundation of a beautiful life for ourselves and others.

The gnome children portrayed in this card are busily creating a home with various tools and a cooperative spirit. The foundation for this house is an apple tree, signifying the Tree of Life. In Greek myth, the apple tree is a symbol of abundance.

A new consciousness is being built. In Thailand, many people creating houses construct replicas of those structures, to be inhabited by spirits. These miniature models are called "houses of spirits." This ancient practice welcomes guardian angels into the households and fashions talismans for the overlighting power of universal love and truth. From the awareness achieved with this practice, family members can develop inner strength and reverence for all life.

These gnomes are very focused. Their work is taken seriously. They hold a vision that they are in a process of manifesting. What in your life is being built? What inner vision do you carry? Whatever it may be, concentration, responsibility, devotion, and diligence are the four corners you must construct in order to accomplish your true goals.

Five of Crystals

Five of Crystals

In this card, a wise grandpa gnome is placing the final touches on a sacred mandala perched at the top of a tree house. There are two aspects to the mandala's design: a pentacle and golden circles. The circles and the star together in one pattern indicate the union of Earth and heaven. The five points of the star represent birth, initiation, service, rest, and transformation. This symbol is used as a beautiful emblem or stained-glass motif for a home because it represents the evolution of humanity and is a protective shield.

Grandpa gnome whistles a happy tune, for he has manifested a vision of beauty. The apples on the tree are ripe, revealing the fruition of a task well done. The birds convey the rewards of spiritual freedom that come from a well-constructed life.

Fully embrace the gifts offered in this card. Remember to pick the ripe potentials that life reveals to you at this time. Let them manifest. Creativity is at the core of your existence. You might like to explore stained-glass work, pottery, woodworking, sewing, or other handicrafts as a new hobby. Above all, as you pursue creative outlets, stay in touch with the wonders of the Earth and all its heavenly beauty.

Six of Crystals

Six of Crystals

The six gnomes in this card have set out together to accomplish a great goal—to reach the top of a mountain. One gnome has reached the summit. Awaiting him is the vision of a radiant snowflake, a six-pointed marvel of nature. The six-pointed star or hexagram is also called "the flower of Aphrodite," "the Star of David," and "the Seal of Solomon." In Pythagorean mathematics, the number 6 is considered the only "perfect" number between one and ten. It signifies divine wisdom, harmony, equilibrium, and balance between the feminine and masculine dimensions of consciousness.

There is a sense of ecstasy in this card because of the ultimate success it portrays. Group work, perseverance, loyalty, and goal orientation are key components as one seeks to reach seemingly impossible heights. The number 6 can refer to peak experiences. It is usually expansive and positive in nature.

When you receive the Six of Crystals, it is a sign to redouble your efforts to achieve important goals. The climb may be steep, but the rewards will be plentiful. Remember to honor the process and have faith in yourself. If your work is humble and carries a purpose beyond yourself, you may expect great fulfillment and happiness in the years to come. On an elevated level, this card depicts global service and the ideal of world harmony, symbolized by the beautiful snowflake.

Seven of Crystals

Seven of Crystals

The lighting of a candle is a symbolic gesture. It represents a time to usher in the illumination of the soul. The winter solstice is a sacred turning point of the year and often occurs close to the Hebrew "Festival of Lights," known as Chanukah. At the solstice, there is prayer and celebration honoring the Sun's rebirth and the new dawning of the Higher Self. At this time, one can move away from isolation or darkness, where spiritual seeds are sown, toward light and unity, where the flowers of wisdom can blossom.

The young gnome girl in this card is creating a sanctuary for herself, a place where she can go within and seek inner peace, clarity, and vision. She is experiencing a period of contemplation in which she can reach into the depths of her personal knowledge in order to weave truth and wisdom into light. Inner transformation is represented by the rainbow carpet on which she kneels. The seven candles are like a menorah. They symbolize "lamps" or "guides" that help illuminate the process.

A time of waiting or rest is offered to you. Let these candle lights reflect the brilliance of your inner journey. Find your own attunement and trust that all is well. Patience is a cardinal virtue. This may be a time to pause or a phase when you are rebuilding strength for your next adventure or awareness in life. Be still and let the inner truth be revealed.

Eight of Crystals

Eight of Crystals

The precision of a figure skater is inspiring to watch. The time and practice that must be devoted to the sport are apparent when one sees the grace and form demonstrated by a skater on the frozen surface. As the skater glides and dances on the ice, it appears as if he or she has united with a band of angels, joyfully spinning in the cosmic vortex of life. The figure skater exemplifies a perfect union or balance between nature and humanity.

Deep-seated changes and transformation–represented by the number 8—occur for the dedicated individual who achieves excellence in a specialized talent. At this level of inspiration, the influence of greatness affects the greater community. This is the ultimate use of skills that can transfigure the world. When individuals are willing to strive for success in the fields of art, education, and social service, humanity begins to fulfill its potential as a custodian of divine love and wisdom on our planet.

The child skater on this card is creating a figure eight, the ancient symbol of infinity (often drawn as a double-coiled serpent biting its own tail). In the Eight of Crystals, the pattern represents the infinite potential of the human being. When this card appears in your reading, look into the deeper realms of your life to discover the gifts that you can share with the world. Allow your hidden skills and creative abilities to fully manifest.

Nine of Crystals

Nine of Crystals

A fire is brilliantly glowing inside the gnome cottage on this card as the thrill and anticipation of Christmas Eve fill the air. A stage of completion draws near. Much preparation has gone into creating a festive and warm holiday. The gestating hope and wonder of gifts yet to come instill a sense of awe as Christmas morning draws near. The mama gnome is pregnant, and her candle symbolizes the light of the new soul about to be born. Presents under the tree remain unopened, and the stockings on the hearth are not yet filled. The nine stockings over the fire represent a profound receptivity to higher forces, while the nine candles illuminating the beautiful yule tree turn it into a glowing crystal. The little gnome girl anticipates the arrival of Saint Nicholas, yet she knows she must sleep and surrender to another world of dreams before his magical offering will come. Expectation abounds.

The Nine of Crystals marks the period of life when the divine potential of the future is near. The mama gnome is reading a story to her child. When you receive this card, realize that you are also meant to be the storyteller of your life. The story can be only as conscious as the one who tells it. What new theme, fairy tale, or adventure will you enter into next? As you move into this period of completion, trust in the goodness of what is yet to manifest in your life. A magical gift, a special friendship, or a new opportunity may be on its way.

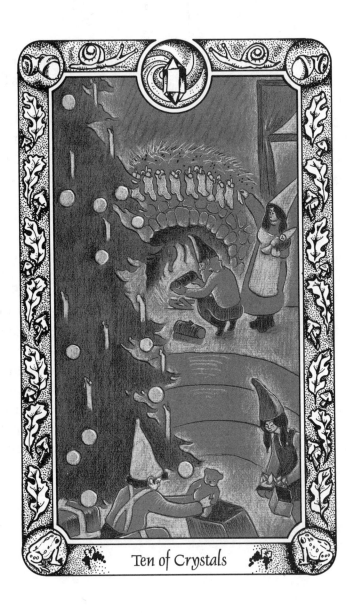

Ten of Crystals

Ten of Crystals

Christmas Day carries the potential for great joy and expectations. Dreams may come true, and the rekindling of family ties and friendly sharings brings warmth and love into the home. In this card, all of the stockings have been filled and a tiny one is being hung to celebrate the birth of the baby gnome. Papa gnome lights the yule log to promote the light and joy of this family and community gathering. All of the gifts have been opened, and the children gaze in delight at the treasures they have received. The girl gnome sits on a rainbow carpet while she looks at a wondrous crystal. The day is bright, the Sun is high, and the family rejoices.

Let the scene in the Ten of Crystals warm your heart. Celebrations and festivals of all traditions bring people together. They instill a special feeling of gratitude that comes from the desire to be universally connected and loved. Open to the gifts that life has in store for you. You may want to reacquaint yourself with ancient rituals and blessings that can spark new fires in your creative imagination. Your healing prayers and thoughts can uplift many people around the globe. Remember to aid the disadvantaged and homeless, who may be downcast and in need of a helping hand. Be thankful for all the blessings offered to you by angels, invisible helpers, and higher teachers throughout your lifetime.

Child of Crystals

Child of Crystals
Huck Finn

The Child of Crystals, represented by Mark Twain's delightful character Huck Finn, is the untamed part of us that desires adventure and an uncivilized relationship with the Earth. In the beginning stages of consciousness, we are introduced to the concepts of abundance, honesty, boundaries, experimentation, and responsibility on the physical plane. How we deal with these attributes has a direct bearing on our maturation beyond the child state of existence.

Huck Finn is the proverbial vagabond boy, the son of the town drunk who rebels against the dictates of social convention. During Huck's adventures on the Mississippi River, many symbolic issues arise concerning freedom—his own and the freedom of black slave Jim—and the quest for higher life. The issue of the wise use of earthly resources is presented when Huck and his companion Tom Sawyer find money that robbers have hidden in a cave. They get six thousand dollars apiece as a reward, all in gold. The judge allows them to have a dollar a day. Huck's life is one of wit, trial and error, and the desire to remain a child at heart. Ultimately, we can identify with Huck's resistance to growing up as he experiences obstacles and triumphs throughout his initiation into adulthood. Huck Finn is a reminder of the earthy soul within ourselves. He is a mirror reflection of nature's wildness and the independent spirit personified by the great god of the pagan world Pan.

In the Child of Crystals card, Huck is fishing in the Mississippi on a lazy summer's day. One might say that he is fishing for new knowledge in the wisdom stream of humanity's consciousness. As the Child of Crystals, he has his various animal friends, his trusty slingshot, and a calmness that reminds us of the harmonious vibrations of Mother Nature.

When Huck appears for you, let your adventurous spirit roam free. Hike through the woods. Leave the world of civilization for the great outdoors. Paddle your canoe downstream. Ask yourself some hard questions about your personal freedom, your use of physical gifts with sensitivity and skill, and any fears you may have about being a responsible member of society. Try to fathom where you are now along the meandering river of life.

Seeker of Crystals

Seeker of Crystals
The Cowardly Lion

We are all learning about the tremendous amount of courage required to face obstacles along the path of life. As we travel into the future, let us remember the story of the Cowardly Lion in *The Wizard of Oz*. Dorothy finds him in the woods, seemingly very defensive and self-assured. When the lion's scary tactics don't work, he is confronted with his own fears and vulnerabilities. He sets off to see the Wizard with Dorothy, the Tin Man, and the Scarecrow to acquire some courage.

As the story unfolds, the lion transforms himself through bravery in order to save Dorothy from the Wicked Witch. As in many fables and fairy tales, his courage and magnificent true self emerge on the journey as he is asked to serve and protect his beloved companions. His earlier façade is no longer needed as he faces life-threatening situations in which truth, valor, and honor are required.

In the Seeker of Crystals card, the Cowardly Lion is traveling on the Yellow Brick Road and receiving a garland of flowers to crown his achievements. There is a strong rapport between this image and the Beauty and the Beast Trump card. If both cards do come up in a reading, it is indicative of a major lesson about spiritual empowerment.

When the Cowardly Lion appears for you, remember to tap into your hidden strength and power. Sometimes this power must be expressed in a gentle manner; other times it should be revealed in a fiercely passionate way. The false pride and selfishness that you may project out of fear and doubt are best replaced with an honorable willingness to feel your own pain. Let the inner truth of your radiant soul come shining through. Just like the Cowardly Lion, you will be crowned with a victor's wreath denoting glory and hard-won accomplishments.

Guide of Crystals

Guide of Crystals
St. Nicholas

While Santa Claus appears to be a culturally bound persona whose presence has degenerated into rampant materialism, the true essence of Saint Nicholas and Santa Claus has its source in the divine origins of our planet. In esoteric circles, the name for the "ruler of the Earth" is said to be Sanat Kumara. This being is considered to be the Lord of the World, whose mirror reflection may be Lucifer, the fallen angel, or Satan. Notice that the names *Santa* and *Satan* are anagrams of *Sanat*. Each word has five letters, and the numerical value of each name is 55.

The upright five-pointed star is, in occult traditions, symbolic of a human being evolving toward spiritual enlightenment. Every human soul is a miniature star: the human head, two arms, and two legs represent a fivefold expression of this soul in the world. As Sanat Kumara presides over our planet from invisible levels of being, Santa Claus—the Lord of the North Pole (spiritual "head center" or intake valve for the Earth)—is the legendary or mythic expression of this being. The true Sanat Kumara works behind the scenes to protect and nurture humanity.

Historically, there was a Saint Nicholas, born in the fourth century A.D. to a wealthy family living in Asia Minor. He became known for his holiness, miracles, and zeal. He was also imprisoned for his Christian faith. Part of his life's purpose was to convert sinners, share his wealth with the poor, and increase charity among the populace. Eventually, he came down to us as the patron of storm-ravaged sailors, prisoners, and children. Because of his generosity, children began giving gifts at Christmastime, and his name was metamorphosed into Santa Klaes and Santa Claus by the Dutch.

The image of Santa Claus with a flowing white beard pictured on the Guide of Crystals card is similar to the image of Grandfather Time, the keeper of hopes and dreams who holds the key to potential manifestation. The rabbit on the card denotes fertility. Steeped in the suit of Earth Crystals is the message of Earth harvest, growth, productivity, and reproduction. Saint Nicholas is a Minor Arcana version of Trump card V—The Wizard—who bridges the material and spiritual worlds, encouraging us to aspire to the wisdom to create abundance on Earth.

The appearance of this card suggests that you have been blessed in many ways. Explore the well of abundance and kindness that you can draw upon at any time. Expect miracles–the attainment of your wishes is possible. Remember the magic of believing. Rekindle your childlike sense of anticipation. When opportunity knocks, your hopes and prayers may be answered. Be generous. Be kind. Be thankful.

Guardian of Crystals

Guardian
of Crystals
Gaia

Both the Earth Crystal suit and *Inner Child Cards* end with Gaia, the gentle caretaker of planet Earth. She is eternally abundant, reverent, and wise. Her protection extends to the entire human family and all of nature's creatures. She is constantly working to maintain the delicate ecological balance and to reinstate inner harmony within the polluted atmosphere, waters, and soil across the globe. She is sorrowful that humans are destroying the rain forests and exterminating beautiful sea creatures, owls, elephants, and other living beings for their own selfish purposes.

The Guardian of Crystals is a head of state, teacher, politician, lawyer, physician, or spiritual healer at the highest level—someone who holds a universal vision and a panoramic view of life. As the twentieth century closes, many scientists are awakening to a new view of life on planet Earth, suggesting what is called the "Gaia hypothesis." They have finally accepted what millions of spiritually aware people have known for ages: the Earth is a pulsating, living, breathing organism in the cosmos.

In this card, Gaia holds the Earth sphere in her gentle hands, radiating warmth and nurturance. She offers the wisdom of time, reminding us that there is a season for every divine purpose and a meaningful cycle for every earthly transformation. She is the loving presence we may contact when we visit mountains, oceans, waterfalls, gardens, forests, meadows, and canyons. Her greatest strength is felt when the Sun, in opposition to the Earth, moves through Cancer and the Earth travels through Capricorn.

The quartz crystal on a pendant around Gaia's neck suggests the opening of humanity's throat chakra, creating an increased ability for people to communicate globally through newspapers, radio, television, computers, satellites, clairvoyance, and mental telepathy. Gaia is bringing the human family together through a combination of inventive thinking and a back-to-the-land movement that has even surfaced in politics as the Green Party.

When Gaia appears in your reading, be thankful for the gift of life. Treasure your deepest friendships. Give gratitude to the parents and relatives who raised you and to the elders who inspire you with great visions of hope and the triumph of the human spirit. Devote yourself to beautifying and enriching the land. Get involved with recycling, gardening, and planting trees. Donate funds or volunteer your time to an environmental cause. Visit a special nature sanctuary and explore the wisdom teachings that emanate from the heart and soul of the Earth.

Notes

1. The authors are aware of the seemingly negative portrayal of certain female and male roles in fairy tales. Entire books could be written on this subject, but it is beyond the scope of this project to analyze the complexity surrounding this issue. We hope that our readers will search within their own hearts and minds to uncover the deeper symbolism inherent in these images.

2. At this stage it is important to realize that both the tarot and playing cards have "magical" properties—that is, both are systems of higher knowledge and guidance that allow the trained individual to tap into the secrets of the Ageless Wisdom. How is this possible? How does this work?

Writers like Manly Palmer Hall (*The Secret Teachings of All Ages*), Stuart Kaplan (*The Encyclopedia of Tarot*), and others have pointed out that a regular deck of cards seems to reflect the cycles of the year. The fifty-two cards represent the fifty-two weeks in a year. The four suits—two red (hearts and diamonds) and two black (spades and clubs)—symbolize the four seasons. The thirteen cards in each suit stand for the thirteen lunar months in a year. Furthermore, if you add up the numerical values for each of these thirteen cards, you will come up with the number 91 for each suit. If you then multiply 91 by 4 (the number of suits), you come up with 364. Add the Joker and you have the 365 days in a year. Clearly then, modern playing cards have a deep and mysterious connection with cosmic cycles. In most situations, in the hands of a carnival-type magician or gypsy fortune teller, modern playing cards will not "speak to the soul" of an individual looking for divine inspiration. But we should accept the fact that modern playing cards, when used correctly, can be a source of spiritual insight.

3. This link between the numbers *1, 3, 7,* and *22* is expressed in another truly mind-illuminating way. The mathematical term *pi*—the universally constant relationship between the diameter and the circumference of a circle—when shown as a decimal number is written 3.14159. . . (the number sequence goes on to infinity). However, to the ancients, pi was expressed as a fraction: 3 1/7. This fraction can also be changed simply into 22/7. Somehow, the numbers representing pi are a kind of secret formula that expresses the world of spiritual power and unity (1), creativity and the divine trinity (3), worldly expression (7), and human attainment (22). The twenty-two cards of the Major Arcana are a type of imaginative and psychic pi, revealing the circular and cyclical magic of human life, death, and reincarnation.

Even when we investigate the very air we breathe on this planet, we note an extraordinary numerological link to the tarot. Earth's atmosphere by volume is composed of 78 percent nitrogen, 21 percent oxygen, and 1 percent other gases like helium, argon, and so on. Once again, we are confronted by a mystery of nature: the percentage of nitrogen equals the number of cards in the tarot; the percentage of oxygen (necessary for human survival) equals the twenty-one numbered cards of the Major Arcana; and the percentage of other gases, the unusual "extra something" in the air, equals one card, The Fool (0).

The more we study the system of tarot, the more we realize that it is a universal presence throughout our lives:

in the air we breathe, in our DNA and genes, and in the origins of our alphabet.

4. Philip M. Chancellor, *Dr. Philip M. Chancellor's Handbook of the Bach Flower Remedies* (New Canaan, CT: Keats Publishing, 1980): p.13.

Bibliography

Bettelheim, Bruno. *The Uses of Enchantment: The Meaning and Importance of Fairy Tales.* New York: Vintage Books, 1977.

Burnham, Sophy. *A Book of Angels: Reflections on Angels Past and Present and True Stories of How They Touch Our Lives.* New York: Ballantine Books, 1990.

Butler, Bill. *Dictionary of the Tarot.* New York: Schocken Books, 1975.

Campbell, Joseph, and Richard Roberts. *Tarot Revelations.* San Anselmo, CA: Vernal Equinox Press, 1987.

Case, Paul Foster. *The Tarot: A Key to the Wisdom of the Ages.* Richmond, VA: Macoy Publishing Company, 1947.

Chancellor, Philip M. *Dr. Philip M. Chancellor's Handbook of the Bach Flower Remedies.* New Canaan, CT: Keats Publishing, 1980.

Clow, Barbara Hand. *Chiron: Rainbow Bridge Between the Inner and Outer Planets.* St. Paul: Llewellyn Publications, 1987.

Hall, Manly P. *An Encyclopedic Outline of Masonic, Hermetic, Qabbalistic and Rosicrucian Symbolical Philosophy: Being an Interpretation of the Secret Teachings concealed within the Rituals, Allegories and Mysteries of all Ages.* Los Angeles: Philosophical Research Society, 1977.

Kaplan, Stuart R. *The Encyclopedia of Tarot*. Vol. 1. New York: U.S. Games Systems, Inc., 1978.

Lotterhand, Jason C. *The Thursday Night Tarot: Weekly Talks on the Wisdom of the Major Arcana*. North Hollywood, CA: Newcastle Publishing, 1989.

Meyer, Rudolf. *The Wisdom of Fairy Tales*. Hudson, NY: Anthroposophic Press, 1988.

Nichols, Sallie. *Jung and Tarot: An Archetypal Journey*. York Beach, ME: Samuel Weiser, 1980.

Noble, Vicki. *Motherpeace: A Way to the Goddess Through Myth, Art, and Tarot*. San Francisco: Harper & Row, 1983.

Saint-Exupéry, Antoine de. *The Little Prince*. Translated by Katherine Woods. New York: Harcourt, Brace & World, 1943.

Tolkien, J.R.R. *The Lord of the Rings*. New York: Ballantine Books, 1967.

Walker, Barbara G. *The Woman's Dictionary of Symbols and Sacred Objects*. San Francisco: Harper & Row, 1988.

About the Authors

Isha Lerner has been working with and studying astrology, tarot, and the healing arts since the early 1970s. For several years while in the Hawaiian Islands and later at the Findhorn Foundation in Forres, Scotland, she lived in attunement with the nature spirits and elemental life forces of the land. Her deep love of nature and fairy tales, combined with her experience as a mother and as a professional astrologer, inspired her to co-create *Inner Child Cards* with Mark Lerner.

Isha lives in Eugene, Oregon, where she works as a counselor integrating astrology, tarot, fairy tales, and flower-essence therapy into her practice. She has been a staff member of and writer for *Welcome To Planet Earth* magazine since 1981. She can be contacted at the address on the following page for workshops, lectures, and classes.

Mark Lerner graduated from Michigan State University in 1971 with a bachelor in social science. He started his astrological work, metaphysical studies, and explorations into the tarot in New York City in 1972. There he joined the Arcane School, started an astrological practice, and eventually worked at the Lucis Trust, the center for the Alice

 Bailey books and teachings. From 1976 to 1979, he was a member of the Findhorn Foundation in Northern Scotland.

Since 1979, Mark has given slide shows on planetary cycles, had a daily radio show in Madison, Wisconsin, and has been interviewed on radio and television. He began publishing *Welcome To Planet Earth* as a newsletter in 1981; it is now a monthly astrological magazine with thousands of readers.

Mark has extensively researched the correlations between tarot, astrology, fairy tales, psychology, and healing. He began his work with Isha Lerner and Christopher Guilfoil on *Inner Child Cards* in 1988.

To contact Isha or Mark, or to be on their mailing lists, please write to them at the following address:

Welcome To Planet Earth
P.O. Box 5164
Eugene, OR 97405

About the Artist

Christopher Guilfoil was born in Munich, Germany, in 1956. He currently lives and works in the Pacific Northwest with his wife, Ellen, their two lop-eared rabbits, two goldfish, and a dachshund named Willy.